THE WELL-TEMPERED CRITIC

Northrop Frye

The Well-Tempered Critic

Fitzhenry & Whiteside

Published in Canada by

Fitzhenry & Whiteside
195 Allstate Parkway
Markham, Ontario L3R 4T8

Canadian Cataloguing in Publication Data

Frye, Northrop, 1912-
  The well-tempered critic

ISBN 0-88902-746-3

1. Style, Literary - Addresses, essays, lectures.
2. Criticism - Addresses, essays, lectures. I. Title.

PN203.F7 1983   801'.9   C84-098012-4

The quotation, "The Cobra," by Ogden Nash, on pages 70–71, is reprinted by permission of Little, Brown and Company. The selection from *Under Milk Wood,* on page 65, is reprinted by permission of New Directions, Publishers, copyright 1954 by New Directions. *Lilacs* by Amy Lowell is quoted by permission of Houghton Mifflin Company. The passage from *Ulysses* by James Joyce on page 23 is quoted by permission of Random House, Inc. and The Bodley Head Ltd.

THIS BOOK HAS BEEN PUBLISHED WITH THE ASSIST-
ANCE OF A GRANT FROM THE FORD FOUNDATION

TO JAY MACPHERSON

Contents

*T*his book consists of the lectures delivered at the University of Virginia in March, 1961, for the Page-Barbour Foundation, with some expansion and revision. I am indebted to my friends and hosts at the University of Virginia, especially Professor Arthur Stocker, for many kindnesses.

For the convenience of the reader, I have altered the lecture format into a sequence of chapters. These chapters, like the lectures which they originally were, are intended to fit inside one another, like the boxes of Silenus. The first picks up a common problem in the teaching of English and pursues it to a point at which it is seen to be an aspect of a technical problem in the theory of literary criticism. The second attempts to work out the implications of this theory, and the third is concerned with the implications of critical theory itself, thus returning to the social and educational area in which the discussion began.

Readers of my Anatomy of Criticism *will notice that the second chapter attempts to reshape, in a slightly simpler form, some of the distinctions made in the fourth essay of that book. Some of my reviewers felt that I had dismissed Arnold's "touchstone" technique too brusquely, though what I had intended to dismiss was not the technique itself, but a social and moral motivation for it which seemed to me to have a misleading influence on criticism. In my discussion of "high style" I make some effort to indicate what I think the importance of Arnold's conception to be.*

N. F.

1. The Moral of Manner

W E ARE told that in the early days of key-
board instruments it was customary to tune
one scale, usually C major, perfectly, so that whatever was written in that key, or in closely related
keys, would sound beautiful and harmonious. But
this system restricted the number of keys a composer could use; for a key as remote from C major
as, say, G sharp minor, would, at least to a profes-
sional ear, sound like a tree full of starlings. So
a compromise was reached: it was pretended that
the octave could be divided evenly into twelve

13

semitones, and that C sharp and D flat, for instance, were the same note. These assumptions were not exactly true, but they were practical. They enabled a composer to use all twenty-four keys, as Bach's *Well-Tempered Clavichord* twice demonstrates, and even the ears that could notice the difference were approximately satisfied.

It seems to me that there is a parable in this for literary critics. Literary criticism is an outgrowth of literary scholarship: it has the same kind of interest but extends over a much wider field. The scholar, as distinct from the critic, is confined to a relatively small area of literature: he edits Lydgate and becomes known as a Lydgate man, or, if sufficiently distinguished, the Lydgate man. He tunes his own scale as accurately as possible, and on all subjects closely related to Lydgate his utterance is beautiful and harmonious. But it is possible for even a good scholar to be an ill-tempered critic, in the musical sense, because the study of literature lacks any real co-ordinating critical principles. Our university teachers, as scholars, have been trained in a graduate school: as critics, they are largely self-educated. They may never have been confronted with a "survey" of literature which really surveyed anything except chronology, or "tradition," as it is often called. Usually they do a fair job of educating themselves, for after all they must teach, and teaching in the universities is also a self-educating process. But one wonders if there is a way to make the study of criticism one of composition rather than only of improvisation.

For some years I have been in search of the coordinating principles that would make it possible for a student of literature to be trained in criticism as well as in scholarship: to specialize, say, in Chaucer and still be able to modulate to the key of Dostoievsky or Plato, to understand that literature is a coherent order of words and not what Pope calls a wild heap of wit. Such an enlarged perspective may result in some over-simplifying, but, as in equal temperament, there is much to be said for compromise. A few things have become clearer to me as I have proceeded. Of these, one of the most important to me has been the realization that the problems of literary criticism and literary education are inseparable. For the critic's more comprehensive approach to literary problems immediately divides in two. One group of problems is purely critical, and relates to the study of literature as a whole. The other group is cultural, in Arnold's sense, and is concerned with society's use of the art of words, with the general social level of reading, writing and speaking. Its direction is toward what interests the critic as a teacher, seeing what his students do with what he gives them, or simply toward what interests him as a social being, seeing what happens, or fails to happen, in society as a result of his contribution to it. I shall begin by trying to locate one or two of the links between criticism and education, leaving the more technical literary questions for the next chapter.

It is a well known principle of thought that the most elementary problems are the hardest, not only to solve, but even to see. The other day an inspector of elementary schools said to me: "In grade four nearly all the children are enthusiastic about poetry: in the adult world hardly anyone bothers to read it. What happens?" This question struck me as a perversion of nature: everybody knows that literary critics are supposed to ask searching questions of educators, not the other way round. The conviction that I ought to be asking the question, however, clearly would not supply me with an answer. There are any number of automatic or cliché answers, ranging from "Schoolteachers kill the child's interest in poetry by analyzing it" to "Modern poetry is out of touch with modern life"; but such pseudo-statements, however consoling, get us nowhere.

While I do not have an answer, I can at least see the place at which the answer must start. Here again an educational problem is bound up with a critical one. Very early in our education we are made familiar with the distinction between verse and prose. The conviction gradually forces itself on us that when we mean what we say we write prose, and that verse is an ingenious but fundamentally perverse way of distorting ordinary prose statements. The conviction does not come to us from school so much as from the general pressure of our social environment. Embedded in it is the purely critical assumption that prose is the language of ordinary speech. This is an assumption of very long standing: one of the most reliable jokes in literature concerns the delight of M. Jourdain, in Molière's *Le Bourgeois Gentilhomme,* at discovering that he had been speaking prose all his life. But M. Jourdain had not been speaking prose all his life, and prose is not the language of ordinary speech. In the history of literature we notice that developed techniques of verse normally precede, sometimes by centuries, developed techniques of prose. How could this happen if prose were really the language of ordinary speech?

The language of ordinary speech is called prose only because it is not distinguished from prose. Actual prose is the expression or imitation of directed thinking or controlled description in words, and its unit is the sentence. It does not follow that all prose is descriptive or thoughtful, much less logical, but only that prose imitates, in its rhythm and structure, the verbal expression of a conscious and rational mind. Prose, therefore, is not ordinary speech, but ordinary speech on its best behavior, in its Sunday clothes, aware of an audience and with its relation to that audience prepared beforehand. It is the habitual language only of fully articulate people who have mastered its difficult idiom. And even they will avoid stilted speech, or "talking like a book," as we say, and when they do, their speech rhythm shows the influence of something that is not prose.

If we listen to children talking, we do not hear prose: we hear a heavily accented speech rhythm with a great deal of chanting in it, or whining, depending on the mood of the child. If we are lost in a strange town and ask someone for directions, we do not get prose: we get pure Gertrude Stein, a speech rhythm that is prolix and repetitive, and in which the verbal unit is no more a prose sentence than it is a villanelle. The teenager issuing mating calls over a telephone is not speaking prose, although the speech rhythm he uses is as formalized as prayer, which it somewhat resembles. The lady screaming amiabilities at a crowded cocktail party is not allowed to speak prose, for her hearers are not listening for sentences, but for a single rise and fall of the voice. The other day a student came to consult me about a failure in English, and what he said, as I recorded immediately after he left, was this:

Y'know, I couldn' figure what happened, cause, jeez, well, I figured, y'know, I had that stuff cold—I mean, like I say, I'd gone over the stuff an' I figured I knew it, and—well, jeez, I do' know.

I submit that this is not prose, and I suspect he had failed because he had not understood the difficulties of translating his speech into prose. He was, of course, "taking" English. But English was not taking him: fifteen years of schooling had failed to make any impression on his speech habits. He represents an educational problem, but not one that school or university can directly solve, because the only effective improvement would be through social snobbery. If, as at least formerly in England, habits of speech were built into the social structure: if it were taken for granted that the lower classes spoke one way and the middle classes another, middle-class speech would certainly conform to a middle-class pattern from infancy onwards. But Bernard Shaw's *Pygmalion* could hardly be written in North America, for the social facts it deals with are very different here.

Ordinary speech is concerned mainly with putting into words what is loosely called the stream of consciousness: the daydreaming, remembering, worrying, associating, brooding and mooning that continually flows through the mind and which, with Walter Mitty, we often speak of as thought. Thus ordinary speech is concerned mainly with self-expression. Whether from immaturity, preoccupation, or the absence of a hearer, it is imperfectly aware of an audience. Full awareness of an audience makes speech rhetorical, and rhetoric means a conventionalized rhythm. The irregular rhythm of ordinary speech may be conventionalized in two ways. One way is to impose a pattern of recurrence on it; the other is to impose the logical and semantic pattern of the sentence. We have verse when the arrangement of words is dominated by recurrent rhythm and sound, prose when it is dominated by the syntactical relation of subject and predicate. Of the two, verse is much the simpler and more primitive type, which accounts for its being historically earlier than prose.

One can see in ordinary speech, however, a unit of rhythm peculiar to it, a short phrase that contains the central word or idea aimed at, but is largely innocent of syntax. It is much more repetitive than prose, as it is in the process of working out an idea, and the repetitions are largely rhythmical filler, like the nonsense words of popular poetry, which derive from them. In pursuit of its main theme it follows the paths of private association, which gives it a somewhat meandering course. Because of the prominence of private association in it, I shall call the rhythm of ordinary speech the associative rhythm.

Traditionally, the associative rhythm has been used in tragedy to represent insanity, as in some speeches in *King Lear*, and in comedy to represent the speech of the uneducated or the mentally confused. Mrs. Quickly and Juliet's nurse are Shakespearean examples. But it is only within the last century or so, with the rise of mimetic fiction, that literature has made any systematic effort to explore the rhythms of ordinary or of inner speech. Such effort practically begins, for English literature, with the entry of Alfred Jingle into the *Pickwick Papers* and his account of the stage coach and the low archway:

Terrible place—dangerous work—other day—five children—mother—tall lady, eating sandwiches—forgot the arch—crash—knock—children look round—mother's head off—sandwich in her hand—no mouth to put it in—head of a family off—shocking, shocking!

Jingle begins the series of associative speakers that includes the Bloom and Molly Bloom of Joyce's *Ulysses*. Wyndham Lewis, in *Time and*

Western Man, has noted the connection between Jingle and Bloom, although the inferences he draws from the connection are pseudo-critical. Bloom's interior monologue falls into a series of asyntactic phrases, like Jingle's speech, except that the rhythm is a little slower and stodgier, as befits the speaker's physical type:

Confession. Everyone wants to. Then I will tell you all. Penance. Punish me, please. Great weapon in their hands. More than doctor or solicitor. Woman dying to. And I schschschschschsch. And did you chachachachacha? And why did you? Look down at her ring to find an excuse. Whispering gallery walls have ears. Husband learn to his surprise. God's little joke. Then out she comes. Repentance skin deep. Lovely shame. Pray at an altar. Hail Mary and Holy Mary.

Here, however, a further distinction arises. When an author represents a character as speaking or thinking in this way, the author is aware of his audience even if his character is not; consequently he will impose on the speech of that character a third type of conventionalization. Jingle and Bloom are literary comic humors, not people drawn from life, and their monologues are more regularized in rhythm than those of any people resembling them in life would be.

There are, then, three primary rhythms of verbal expression. First, there is the rhythm of prose, of which the unit is the sentence. Second, there is an associative rhythm, found in ordinary speech and in various places in literature, in which the unit is a short phrase of irregular length and primitive syntax. Third, there is the rhythm of a regularly repeated pattern of accent or meter, often accompanied by other recurring features, like rhyme or alliteration. This regularly recurring type of rhythm is what I mean by verse. "Poetry," however indispensable a word in literary criticism, can hardly be used in the technical sense of a verbal structure possessing a regular, recurrent, and in general predictable rhythm. All verse is "poetry" as that word is generally used, except when "poetry" implies a value-judgement. It does not follow that all poetry is verse. Any jingle or doggerel that approximately scans is verse in my sense, however unpoetic: no free verse, such as Whitman's, is verse in my sense, however important as poetry.

All three rhythms are involved in all writing, but one is normally the dominating or organizing rhythm.

II

IDEALLY, our literary education should begin, not with prose, but with such things as "this little pig went to market"—with verse rhythm reinforced by physical assault. The infant who gets bounced on somebody's knee to the rhythm of "Ride a cock horse" does not need a footnote telling him that Banbury Cross is twenty miles northeast of Oxford. He does not need the information that "cross" and "horse" make (at least in the pronunciation he is most likely to hear) not a rhyme but an assonance. He does not need the value-judgement that the repetition of "horse" in the first two lines indicates a rather thick ear on the part of the composer. All he needs is to get bounced. If he is, he is beginning to develop a response to poetry in the place where it ought to start. For verse is closely related to dance and song; it is also closely related to the child's own speech, which is full of chanting and singing, as well as of primitive verse forms like the war-cry and the taunt-song. At school the study of verse is supplemented by the study of prose, and a good prose style in both speech and writing is supposed to be aimed at. But poetry, the main body of which is verse, is always the central powerhouse of a literary education. It contributes, first, the sense of rhythmical energy, the surge and thunder of epic and the sinewy and springing dialogue of Shakespearean drama. It contributes too, as the obverse of this, the sense of leisure, of expert timing of the swing and fall of cadences. Then there is the sense of wit and heightened intelligence, resulting from seeing disciplined words marching along in metrical patterns and in their inevitably right order. And there is the sense of concreteness that we can get only from the poet's use of metaphor and of visualized imagery. Literary education of this kind, its rhythm and leisure slowly soaking into the body and its wit and concreteness into the mind, can do something to develop a speaking and writing prose style that comes out of the depths of personality and is a genuine expression of it.

As education proceeds, the student finds himself surrounded with what purports to be prose, and naturally gives this rhythm more of his attention. Prose becomes the language of information, and it becomes increasingly also the language of information about poetry, which now tends to recede as a direct experience of words. As a result of colliding with *The Lady of the Lake* in grade nine, I shall associate Scott with unmetrical footnotes all my life:

> The stag at eve had drunk his fill
> Where danced the moon on Monan's, one, rill:
> And deep his midnight lair had made
> In lone Glenartney's, two, hazel shade.

I am not disapproving the practice of writing footnotes to the proper names in verse, that being one of the ways by which I make my own living. What I regret is the growth of a tendency to find the footnote easier to read, and which in universities takes the form of dealing with a course in literature by reading books about poetry and skipping the quotations. The process, however, is by no means merely one of transferring literary experience from poetry to prose. What more frequently happens is that, faced with the enormous mass of verbiage on all sides, and having to come to terms with the constant sense of panic that this inspires, the student is taught, or develops by himself, a technique of reading everything quickly and off the top of his head. He no longer responds to the rhythm of the sentence, or to any rhythm at all, but reads with a mechanical express-train efficiency, dealing only with what that kind of efficiency can handle—the main ideas, the gist of the argument, the general point of view, and the like. This means that the process of reading is, like the rhythms of undeveloped speech, becoming purely associative. It is appropriate for a committee's report, or similar expendable document, where there is one essential sentence on page forty-two and the reader wants only to get some notion of its context; but it is inadequate for prose, and impossible for poetry.

Meanwhile, in all the attention put on techniques of teaching students to read, ordinary speech is largely left to original sin. A standard grammatical form of English prose is taught at school, and the student learns to read it after a fashion, but it does not follow that he learns to speak it habitually. Learning to speak on this continent is often associated with "cultivating an accent," and it is generally agreed that anyone who does that is a sissy, a snob, a square, or whatever other abusive term is in vogue at the moment. I am not myself speaking of accent, or of the actual production of the sounds of speech, which is a social convention only. I am speaking of the kind of oral verbal framework that one must develop if one is to convey ideas or communicate any sense of personality. Prose is founded on the sentence, and the sentence is, at least in form, logical, communicable and periodic: it is difficult to use unless one has something to say and means what one says. We notice that associative speakers have a great aversion to the definiteness and full close of the sentence: if they produce a sentence by accident, they will add unnecessary words to the end as an apology for having uttered it, like.

On my desk is the report of a conference transmitted by that sobering register of the spoken word, the tape recorder. The question at issue is the teaching of American literature in foreign countries: *Huckleberry Finn* has been suggested, and the speaker is, I think, warning us that it contains the word "ain't":

Now, I'm rather more inclined to stick my neck out on things of this sort, therefore, I'm sticking my neck farther than a lot of people here would, in saying that I would also not see any objection to including such a supposedly sub-standard term as ain't in the sense of am not, is not, are not at a relatively early level of work for teaching English, but in this case with a specific indication that this is an extremely frequent form which the learner is very likely to hear in any part of the English speaking world but that he had better be careful about using it himself unless he has more of a feel for the situations in which it is permissible and those in which it "ain't."

This kind of style, once one gets more of a feel for it, is easy to recognize as the quiz programme or buzz session style. Its unit is not the sentence, but the number of words that it is possible to emit before someone else breaks in. A discussion based on such a speech rhythm cannot achieve conversation, but only distributed monologue.

The schools, of course, will be of little help if they have been corrupted by project methods and other anti-verbal perversities. If a standard language is taught in school without conviction, it is unlikely to make much positive impression on the language spoken during recess. I say positive impression, because there does seem to be a negative one. Much of the colloquial language spoken in our society is a curious mixture of associative monologue and childhood resentments. I often revert to a little scene that made a considerable impression on me once: in a grocery store, where the clerk was showing me two things much alike, he remarked: "It doesn't make any difference," then looked me full in the face and instantly corrected himself to: "It don't make no difference." This second form was an improvement on the first, having a higher degree of what literary critics call texture. It meant (a) it doesn't make any difference (b) you look to me like a schoolteacher, and nobody's going to catch me talking like one of them. If he said: "It don't make no difference," it was not because he did not know the accepted form, but because he did know it. His speech was not ungrammatical; it was anti-grammatical. Whatever unconscious resentment may be involved in such rhetoric is not directed against a higher social class: it is directed against eggheads or longhairs or however the people are described who take their education seriously. The language taught at school is taught only there, which is why it is associated with teachers and schoolrooms. It would never have occurred to the student whose ragged speech I have quoted to be anything but clean and well dressed. But no major business is engaged in selling speech, and the example of good speakers is not reinforced by advertising, with its judicious mixture of flattery and threats.

The standard English of schoolrooms is prose, and being prose it can be analyzed grammatically, hence the body of grammatical "rules" which so many students associate with correct English. When anyone starts reflecting, as I am doing, on ordinary habits of speech, it is usually assumed that it is the correctness of one's grammar that is being impugned. But while standard speech is grammatical, it would be silly to judge it solely by its conformity to some alleged grammatical model. For one thing, the strain of constructing prose sentences is clearly marked even in the speech of the most articulate people. That is to say, the point I want to make is, all of us use, sort of, filler phrases to conceal our nervousness, or something, in working out our, you know, sentence structure. Standard English cannot be learned without the study of formal grammar. The little learning of linguistics which prompted some "educators" a few years ago to try to get rid of grammar proved to be a very dangerous thing indeed. Further, those who know language know its logical distinctions and subtle nuances, and have a duty to insist on their usefulness. The notion that the teacher of language has nothing to do but follow "usage" is one of the more miserable forms of academic self-deprecation. But still grammar is the servant and not the master of language, and speech, like handwriting, has to be allowed to find its own rhythm and character.

The hazy general notion that illiteracy is the technical inability to read and write, and that an education which teaches everybody to read and write has overcome illiteracy, is clearly nonsense. One may fully agree with everything that has been said about the futility of teaching dead languages at school. Except for some aspects of scholarly research, dead languages have no place in education. But this does not commit us to making the simple-minded and ill-considered identification of dead languages with the Classical languages. A dead language is a language that one learns to read but never thinks of as spoken. What shows that it is dead is the third factor, the writing of the language. The professor of Latin does not think of Latin as a dead language except when he is marking students' proses. Similarly, a student who has learned to read English prose, and continues to speak only associative jargon, will, when he tries to write English, find himself struggling with a language much more effectively dead than Julius Caesar. Good writing must be based on good speech; it will never come alive if it is based on reading alone.

Many people are puzzled by the fact that only the most disciplined writers are simple writers. Undeveloped writing is not simple, even in the sense of reproducing the associative speech patterns that I have quoted earlier. Writing that did that would achieve, if not simplicity, at least a kind of startling nakedness. Such writing is to be found in examination papers, of the sort that exclude their authors from a university education. Here is an example at random, from a student who was asked to compare Chaucer's Chanticleer with one of the characters in the General Prologue:

The discription of the cock is like that of the Prioress, for we are told lots about her appearance, just as of the cock. The discription is general, typical of a Prioress, just as the discription is typical of a cock. We are told that she also could sing good, just as the cock. We know she was beautiful and care much about her manners. This is funny, for a prioress should not be concerned with such, but should pay more attention to her religion. It is funny. The discription of the cock being beautiful is also funny, especially the part about his nails compaired to a lilly. He is interested in love, having seven hens, and so is the Prioress . . .

Everybody engaged in teaching has marked bushels of such offerings: my only purpose in quoting it is to call attention to the murmuring, repetitive, asyntactic phrasing of the rhythm of association. But associative speakers are largely unaware of their own speech habits, and unless they are as naive as this student, they do not use them as a basis for writing. Now if we write in a way that we never speak, the first thing that disappears is the rhythm. It is hardly possible to give any spring or bounce to words unless they come out of our own bodies and are, like dancing or singing, an expression of physical as well as mental energy. The second thing that disappears is the color. It is hardly possible to use vivid language unless one is seeing the imagery for oneself: even abstract words, if they are genuinely possessed by the person using them, will still retain something of the concrete metaphor that they originally had. The third thing that disappears is the sense of personality, which only a basis in personal speech can ever supply. These are all, we have said, the results of a literary education centered in poetry. It is natural that associative speakers, for whom even English prose is a dead language, should regard English poetry with the baffled stare of a stranger accosted by a lunatic. I suspect that much of the difficulty complained of in contemporary poetry is really due to its use of simple and concrete language.

I feel, therefore, that there is a close connection among three aspects of language in our society. First is the associative squirrel-chatter that one hears on streets, and even in college halls, jerking along apologetically or defiantly in a series of unshaped phrases, using slang or vogue words for emphasis and punctuation. Second is the poetic illiteracy which regards anything in verse as a verbal puzzle, not even a puzzle to be worked out, but a disdainful and inscrutable puzzle without an answer. Third is the dead, senseless, sentenceless, written pseudo-prose that surrounds us like a boa constrictor, which is said to cover its victims with slime before strangling them. This last, under the names of jargon, gobbledygook, and the like, has often enough been recognized as a disease of contemporary language and ridiculed or deplored as such.

Two features of pseudo-prose seem to me of particular importance. One is that colorless and rhythmless writing is designed to obliterate the sense of personality: we write this way when we want to speak with some kind of impersonal or anonymous voice. It is not a healthy tendency, for, as Kierkegaard reminds us, the impersonal (in this context) is essentially demoralizing. The other is its underlying assumption that the idea is substantial and that the words which express the idea are incidental. This is a fallacy developed from the habit of associative reading. The words used are the form of which the ideas are the content, and until the words have been found, the idea does not fully exist. It seems to me that the fallacy of the substantial idea has a great deal to do with the bewildering woolliness of so much discursive writing today where (as in literary criticism, philosophy and much of the social sciences) the essential conceptions are verbal rather than mathematical, as mathematical language is doubtless used more accurately.

Elsewhere on my desk, which is a very untidy one, I find the following:

In matters of curriculum, textbooks, or methods of study, variety is the spice of education and decentralization can be even more readily provided than under the small unit system because the resultant stability of teaching personnel means that the central authorities no longer have to keep so tight a grip upon a shifting texture of educational personnel.

The clanging repetition of "personnel" and the huddle of mixed metaphors at the end indicate that the author is writing in his sleep, and there is the usual absence of rhythm and color. But here we notice something else: the cliché or ready-made phrase ("variety is the spice of education") is beginning to make itself felt as a unit of thought and expression. A student of mine recently found herself at a conference of people who write (and talk) like this, and came back muttering a sentence that had, understandably, got stuck in her mind: "Jobwise, are we structured for this activation?" What is striking about this sentence is that it consists entirely of ready-made vogue or jargon words. The cliché is no longer an occasional resource: it has taken over as the only form of expression, and consequently as the only form of thought. A century ago Flaubert explored, with horrified fascination, the cultural life of Bouvard and Pécuchet, whose intellects moved entirely within the orbit of what he drew up as a supplement to his research, the Dictionary of Accepted Ideas. But Bouvard and Pécuchet were still a long way from the verbal automatism, a language based on the conditioned reflex, that we have reached with this sentence. The similar jargon used in Marxist countries looks more philosophical at first glance, but it comes from the same part of the nervous system.

III

OUR present subject is rhetoric, or the social aspect of the use of language, and rhetoric from the beginning has been divided into three levels, high, middle and low. These levels were originally suggested by the three classes of society, and are illustrated both in speech and in literature. In literature, for example, Milton employs the low style in some of his prose pamphlets when he is abusing somebody (e.g., *Colasterion*); the middle style in *Paradise Regained,* which is a quietly reflective poem, and the high style when dealing with Satan, the prince of darkness being a gentleman. At present we are concerned with ordinary speech: the literary aspect of the problem will confront us next.

I should like to suggest another way of looking at these traditional rhetorical terms, a way which does not use the misleading analogy of social classes, and which also tries to avoid some of the metaphors lurking in the words "high" and "low." In ordinary speech we can see clearly enough what the middle style is: it is what in Greek is called *koiné,* the ordinary speaking style of the articulate person, and its basis is a relaxed and informal prose, that is, prose influenced by an associative rhythm. It is the language of what ordinarily passes for thought and rational discussion, or for feelings that are communicable and in proportion to their objects. There is also, in North America, a "low," a colloquial or familiar style, which is in the general area of what Mencken calls the vulgate. This is often thought of as merely substandard or illiterate speech, but perhaps it should be regarded simply as a separate rhetorical style, appropriate for some situations and not for others. With all its anti-grammatical forms, it has its own vocabulary, its own syntax, its own rhythm, its own imagery and humor. It is as capable as any other style of literary expression, as *Huckleberry Finn*, despite its addiction to ain't, abundantly proves. These are both genuine styles, and are quite distinct from the bastard styles we have been discussing, the pseudo-prose and the squirrel-chatter which are parodies of middle and low styles respectively.

I find that I am unable to take the next step without raising a moral distinction. Genuine speech is the expression of a genuine personality. Because it takes pains to make itself intelligible, it assumes that the hearer is a genuine personality too—in other words, wherever it is spoken it creates a community. Bastard speech is not the voice of the genuine self: it is more typically the voice of what I shall here call the ego. The ego has no interest in communication, but only in expression. What it says is always a monologue, though if engaged with others, it resigns itself to a temporary stop, so that the other person's monologue may have its turn to flow. But while it seeks only expression, the ego is not the genuine individual, consequently it has nothing distinctive to express. It can express only the generic: food, sex, possessions, gossip, aggressiveness and resentments. Its natural affinity is for the ready-made phrase, the cliché, because it tends to address itself to the reflexes of its hearer, not to his intelligence or emotions. I am not suggesting that society can do without a great deal of automatic babble on ready-made subjects: I am merely saying that we limit the aspects of our personality that we can express with words if we devote ourselves entirely to such verbal quackery.

If we ask what is the natural way to talk, the answer is that it depends on which nature is being appealed to. Edmund Burke remarked that art is man's nature, that it is natural to man to be in a state of cultivation, and the remark has behind it the authority of our whole cultural and religious tradition. What is true of nature is also true of freedom. The half-baked Rousseauism in which most of us have been brought up has given us a subconscious notion that the free act is the untrained act. But of course freedom has nothing to do with lack of training. We are not free to move until we have learned to walk; we are not free to express ourselves musically until we have learned music; we are not capable of free thought unless we can think. Similarly, free speech cannot have anything to do with the mumbling and grousing of the ego. Free speech is cultivated and precise speech, which means that there are far too many people who are neither capable of it nor would know if they lost it.

A group of individuals, who retain the power and desire of genuine communication, is a society. An aggregate of egos is a mob. A mob can only respond to reflex and cliché; it can only express itself, directly or through a spokesman, in reflex and cliché. A mob always implies some object of resentment, and political leaders who speak for the mob aspect of their society develop a special kind of tantrum style, a style constructed almost entirely out of unexamined clichés. Examples may be heard in the United Nations every day. What is disturbing about the prevalence of bad language in our society is that bad language, if it is the only idiom habitually at command, is really mob language.

What is high style? This is one of the oldest questions in criticism: it would almost be possible to translate the title of Longinus' treatise, *Peri Hypsous*, written near the beginning of the Christian era, by this question. As Longinus recognized, the question has, once again, at least two answers, one for literature and another for ordinary speech. In literature it may be correct to translate Longinus' title as "On the Sublime," and use great passages in Shakespeare or Milton for examples. We shall discuss this problem next. In ordinary speech high style is something else. I should say that it emerges whenever the middle style rises from communication to community, and achieves a vision of society which draws speaker and hearers together into a closer bond. It is the voice of the genuine individual reminding us of our genuine selves, and of our role as members of a society, in contrast to a mob. Such style has a peculiar quality of penetration about it: it elicits a shock of recognition, as it is called, which is the proof of its genuineness. High style in this sense is emphatically not the high-flown style: all ornate language in rhetoric belongs to the middle style, the language of society engaged in routine verbal ritual. Genuine high style is ordinary style, or even low style, in an exceptional situation which gives it exceptional authority. To go at once to the highest example of high style, the sentences of the Sermon on the Mount have nothing in them of the speech-maker's art: they seem to be coming from inside ourselves, as though the soul itself were remembering what it had been told so long ago.

High style in ordinary speech is heard whenever a speaker is honestly struggling to express what his society, as a society, is trying to be and do. It is even more unmistakably heard, as we should expect, in the voice of an individual facing a mob, or some incarnation of the mob spirit, in the death speech of Vanzetti, in Joseph Welch's annihilating rebuke of McCarthy during the McCarthy hearings, in the dignity with which a New Orleans mother explained her reasons for sending her white child to an unsegregated school. All these represent in different ways the authority of high style in action, moving, not on the middle level of thought, but on the higher level of imagination and social vision. The mob's version of high style is advertising, the verbal art of penetrating the mind by prodding the reflexes of the ego. As long as society retains any freedom, such advertising may be largely harmless, because everybody knows that it is only a kind of ironic game. As soon as society loses its freedom, mob high style is taken over by the new masters, to become what is usually called propaganda. Then, of course, the moral effects become much more pernicious. Both advertising and propaganda, however, represent the conscious or unconscious pressure on a genuine society to force it into a mass society, which can only be done by debasing the arts.

The attempt to find a well-tempered criticism in education has led us deep into the structure of society. The teacher of language is popularly supposed to be concerned only with what is called "good grammar," which he regards with great reverence for mysterious cultural reasons. The present argument tries to suggest that the subject is a little more serious than that. Except in the nonverbal arts, like mathematics or music, there are no wordless thoughts, nor can any genuine ideas

be expressed in undeveloped speech or writing.
The undeveloped associative rhythm can only reproduce the associative process: by itself it can
never express thought, much less imagination.
What it can express, and most effectively, is hatred,
arrogance and fear. This makes it a considerable
danger at a time when, though some of us are
afraid of science, we have so much less to fear
from science than from a misuse of words. However uninhibited, it is not free speech, and at a
time when most of us feel rather helpless about
how much we can do in the world, free speech
is the one aspect of a genuine society that we all
hold in our hands, or mouths. What the critic as
a teacher of language tries to teach is not an ele-
gant accomplishment, but the means of conscious
life. Literary education should lead not merely to
the admiration of great literature, but to some possession of its power of utterance. The ultimate aim
is an ethical and participating aim, not an aesthetic
or contemplative one, even though the latter may
be the means of achieving the former. If free
speech is cultivated speech, we should think of
free speech, not merely as an uninhibited reaction
to the social order, a release of the querulous ego,

but as the verbal response to human situations, a response which establishes a context of freedom. The sub-literary associative response is anti-social; the cliché or accepted-idea response is a symptom of social stagnation; the free response, when verbal, is one participating in the lucidity of prose and the energy of verse.

The subject known in English-speaking countries as English has at least three dimensions of existence. It is, in the first place, the language of verbal understanding, the normal means of understanding anything that is not mathematical. Secondly, it is the mother tongue, the means of participating in our own society. Thirdly, it is a division of one of the major arts. The mother tongue is the concern of the practical sense that must take the world as it finds it, and keep the reason and the emotions in balance. Literature is addressed to the imagination, which is concerned, not with the environment directly, but with the world that we construct out of our environment. It is also traditional in literary criticism to distinguish three levels on which words operate. There is the level of speculative reason or knowledge of nature (*quid credas*), the level on which we recognize reality and try to give verbal expression to that recognition. Above this is the practical reason (*quid agas*), which determines a choice of action, where the relevant categories are those of freedom and compulsion. Further above is a vision of the nature and destiny of man and the human situation (*quo tendas*). Whether we associate this top level with religion or not, it is the universe of words, the total structure of man's verbal imagination, the world growing out of the human mind like a plant out of a seed, the imaginatively conceivable human world, Paradise with its excluded demons.

When Raphael is talking to Adam in *Paradise Lost*, Adam's natural curiosity impels him to ask whether the other planets are inhabited. Raphael's reply, which covers an inordinate amount of Book Eight, is an epitome of all bad teaching. Some may say this and some on the other hand may say that; there is much to be said on both sides; there are many books that discuss the matter (though they have not yet been written); the whole subject is very difficult, perhaps insoluble; Adam doesn't need to know the answer anyway because it won't be on his examination—in short, it seems clear that Raphael does not know either and lacks the courage to say so.

Yet there is something to be said for this affable and evasive angelic doctor. Adam's question is asked on the level of speculative or natural knowledge; Raphael is concerned with the higher practical reason which man uses in making decisions affecting his own freedom. Reason, Milton said in *Areopagitica,* is but choosing, a remark which so impressed Milton's God that he does Milton the honor of quoting it in Book Three. Raphael, like many today, feels that there is danger when natural or scientific knowledge outruns the moral maturity which keeps us in control of it. In front of Adam is a crucial test which will determine whether he is to remain free or throw his freedom away, a test for which he must concentrate on the Word of God within undistracted by the works of God without. To prepare him for this test, Raphael brings him knowledge of practical reason in the only form in which such knowledge is appropriate to a free man: the form of parable, addressed to what we should call the imagination. He tells Adam the story of the fall of Satan, and leaves

Adam to make what use he will of the story. Adam, facing his crisis like a practical man, which means having little practical reason and less imagination, finds the story extremely remote compared to the warm and naked beauty of Eve. He falls "against his better knowledge," which means in effect his literary knowledge, and proves incapable of making the turn from life to literature that would have preserved him in the properly cultivated world of Paradise. Paradise thus disappears as an outward environment, but it revives within the mind, as a vision evoked by the Word which had created it in the first place. Hence Satan was wrong or irrelevant when he said "Space may produce new worlds." The only new worlds for man are those which the free and disciplined use of words can help to create.

2. Manual of Style

IN DISCUSSING ordinary speech, we identified three primary verbal rhythms: the verse rhythm dominated by recurring beat, the prose rhythm dominated by the sentence with its subject-predicate relation, and the associative rhythm dominated by the short and irregular phrase. Of these, the verse rhythm belongs, now, entirely to literature, and the prose rhythm both to literature and to ordinary speech. The associative rhythm belongs, in its pure form, to undeveloped ordinary speech or to the representing of such speech in

ordinary speech

fiction or drama; but in a conventionalized form, it can also become a third type of literary rhythm. We have now to study the literary roles of these three rhythms, keeping our eye on the literary aspect of the question of high, middle and low styles that was raised in connection with ordinary speech.

There are many other rhythms in literature besides these three, and if these three really are the primary ones, then the other rhythms are combinations of them, prose influenced by verse, verse influenced by prose, prose or verse influenced in either direction by the associative rhythm. The primary rhythms in themselves are intensely continuous, as we can see in the verse epic, the prose treatise, and such associative monologues as Samuel Beckett's *The Unnamable*. We should expect to find the more discontinuous types of rhythm that predominate in, say, free verse or lyric among these secondary or mixed forms. We are now committed to a survey of the six possible combinations of rhythm, the subject having never to my knowledge been studied synoptically.

Verse, in contrast to prose, employs a number of special devices to mark its repetition, such as rhyme and alliteration. In any normal form of continuous verse the number of such devices is restricted. Homer and Virgil use a quantitative metrical system, a scheme which excludes rhyme. Old English poetry uses an alliterative and accentual system which also excludes rhyme; or at least when rhyme occurs, as occasionally in such late poems as *The Phoenix,* it gives an effect of breakdown. Dryden and Pope use rhyme; consequently they avoid alliteration, except for parody, as in Pope's "Great Cibber's brazen, brainless brothers stand." In normal prose, on the other hand, no such features appear at all, unless by accident. In prose the emphasis falls on the syntactical relations of words, hence the prose writer seeks variety of sound, and the sharp clash of rhyme or alliteration in prose is rejected by the ear at once.

Let us begin with normal prose, the language of exposition and description which can be used for either literary or non-literary purposes. Here is a passage from Darwin's *Origin of Species:*

The great and inherited development of the udders in cows and goats, in countries where they are habitually milked, in comparison with these organs in other countries, is probably another instance of the effects of use. Not one of our domestic animals can be named which has not in some country drooping ears; and the view which has been suggested, that the drooping is due to the disuse of the muscles of the ear, from the animal's being seldom alarmed, seems probable.

I have chosen this passage partly because it is prose at some distance from an associative rhythm. It is, in other words, emphatically written prose: anyone who talked like this would be thought pedantic. Still, it is solidly built in a Victorian model, and does not lack either rhythm or readability. Its rhythm is based on the sentence, and it is readable because that rhythm is consistent. We notice a bit of alliteration in it ("the drooping is due to the disuse"), and the alliteration gives a touch of a slightly more vigorous stress accent. The touch is welcome: Darwin has not tried to avoid it, and such a feature, if it appeared in dull or incompetent prose, would not have such a function. Yet we are confident that it is purely "accidental": if we felt it was deliberate we should be annoyed with Darwin. There is an associative trace with the repetition in "probable": this is not good prose style, but again it is unconscious, and so helps to assure us that we are proceeding with the right kind of scientific caution.

Now let us take a passage from Gibbon's *Decline and Fall of the Roman Empire*:

Every circumstance of the secular games was skilfully adapted to inspire the superstitious mind with deep and solemn reverence. The long interval between them exceeded the term of human life; and as none of the spectators had already seen them, none could flatter themselves with the expectation of beholding them a second time. The mystic sacrifices were performed, during three nights, on the banks of the Tiber; and the Campus Martius resounded with music and dances, and was illuminated with innumerable lamps and torches . . . A chorus of twenty-seven youths, and as many virgins, of noble families, and whose parents were both alive, implored the propitious gods in favour of the present, and for the hope of the rising generation; requesting, in religious hymns, that, according to the faith of their ancient oracles, they would still maintain the virtue, the felicity, and the empire of the Roman people.

This is still expository prose, designed to convey information. But here we are aware of deliberate tricks of style, such as the doubling of adjectives and the antithetical balancing of clauses. If we feel annoyed with these devices, we should avoid reading Gibbon: they are his conventions, inseparable from his kind of readability. Gibbon is writing not direct prose but consciously rhetorical prose; or, as we say, he is a "stylist." The stylizing of his sentences indicates a more self-conscious bid for literary fame. He expects to be read for entertainment, in the genuine sense, as well as instruction, and he expects this quality to keep him alive after his work as a historian has been superseded. As part of this he is asking us to develop a *meditative* interest in the theme of the decline of the world's greatest ancient empire. It is the meditative quality in his work that makes his book a permanent possession of literature and not simply a contribution to scholarship: a quality of wisdom and insight rather than merely of learning, and one which may range in the mood of its expression from solemnity to irony. This meditative quality manifests itself in prose sentences with a distinctive roll in them which is unmistakably metrical. If we stop a sentence of Darwin's in the middle, we feel chiefly that certain words are needed to complete the sense: if we stop a sentence of Gibbon's in the middle, we feel that there is also a rhythmical space to be filled up, as we should if we interrupted the reading of verse.

The rhetorical quality of Gibbon's prose puts him close to oratory, and in oratory, though the controlling form is still prose, the chief appeal is to the emotions or the imagination, so that the meditative element is considerably increased. There is a corresponding increase in the metrical influence, especially in the repetitive passages that form the climaxes of so many orations. In (for instance) the Gettysburg address and in Churchill's 1940 speeches, we see how the sentence rhythm breaks up into balanced clauses, or, in moments of emotional climax, into a series of phrase-units, with a recurring accentual pattern that brings it close to verse. We remember Lincoln's "of the people, by the people, for the people," and Churchill's "We shall fight on the beaches; we shall fight in the hills." Here is a similar example from Samuel Johnson's letter to Chesterfield:

The notice which you have been pleased to take of my labours, had it been early, had been kind; but it has been delayed until I am indifferent, and cannot enjoy it; till I am solitary, and cannot impart it; till I am known, and do not want it.

In more than one sense these are "measured" words. We noticed a similar phrase-unit in the monologues of Jingle and Bloom, but these are quite different in effect, because rhetorical, fully aware of a present and an invisible audience. It is possible, of course, to have a more introverted prose rhetoric with the same kind of rhythm, where the author pretends to be talking to himself but is actually working out a stylistic or rhetorical exercise, as in Sir Thomas Browne's *Urn Burial* or Jeremy Taylor's *Holy Dying*. Oratory and metrical rhythm are as evident in Browne's great meditation on death as they are in a contemporary baroque prose form, the *oraison funèbre* of Bossuet:

The spirits put off their malice with their bodies, and Caesar and Pompey accord in Latin Hell, yet Ajax in Homer endures not a conference with Ulysses; and Deiphobus appears all mangled in Virgil's Ghosts, yet we meet with perfect shadows among the wounded ghosts of Homer.

Oratory, then, and rhetorical prose generally, is one of our secondary or mixed forms, a form of prose which shows a considerable influence from verse. One important influence on English rhetorical prose, Biblical parallelism, is a Hebrew verse form reproduced in prose.

But suppose, now, that a more restless and experimental writer were to take a further step, and produce an extreme form of prose, as strongly affected by the characteristics of verse as it could be and still remain prose. This would give us what is known as euphuism, a form of prose in which all the rhetorical devices of verse, rhyme, alliteration, assonance and a half-metrical balancing of phrases and clauses, are employed. Such a prose would contain all the features that a normal prose writer would do his best to eliminate. Here is a euphuistic sentence from Robert Greene's *Card of Fancy:*

This loathsome life of Gwydonius, was such a cutting corrasive to his father's careful conscience, and such a hapless clog to his heavy heart, that no joy could make him enjoy any joy, no mirth could make him merry, no prosperity could make him pleasant, but abandoning all delight, and avoiding all company, he spent his doleful days in dumps and dolours, which he uttered in these words.

We are not surprised to learn that euphuism is of rhetorical origin, deriving partly from sermons, and a euphuistic story, true to its rhetorical ancestry, tends to keep breaking down into a series of harangues. The passage just quoted, as its final phrase indicates, leads up to a harangue, and in Greene's story the hero and heroine eventually settle down to writing letters at each other, each letter a rhetorical exercise. Thus the increase of meditative and rhetorical elements in metrical prose tends to make for discontinuity. We noticed that "primary" forms of prose and verse, like the treatise and the epic, are continuous. One either reads or does not read the *Origin of Species;* but the *Decline and Fall,* with its greater meditative and literary interest, one can read more discontinuously, stopping here and there or going back, if one is familiar with it, to certain passages. In euphuism the discontinuity has begun to affect the structure.

Along with discontinuity there comes a certain sense of paradox. Euphuism, as we remember from Falstaff, is easy to parody, but in euphuism itself there is a curious quality that is really a kind of self-parody. Its ingenuity makes it witty, and the wit may be conscious or, at times, unconscious: one wonders which it is in Lyly's "which I cannot without blushing behold, or without blubbering utter." Euphuism was an experimental style, and so had its vogue and then quickly went out of fashion, as experimental styles usually do. But what euphuism represents, the ornamenting of a prose rhythm with as many of the features of verse as possible, is a permanent technical resource of style, and will reappear whenever occasion seems to call for it. Here, handled with great tact and skill, is a passage of modern euphuism: the familiar opening of Dylan Thomas's *Under Milk Wood:*

It is Spring, moonless night in the small town, starless and bible-black, the cobblestreets silent and the hunched, courters'-and-rabbits' wood limping invisible down to the sloeblack, slow, black, crowblack, fishingboat-bobbing sea.

When oratorical prose is pushed to the limit of euphuism, an associative element begins to make itself felt in the writing. But here we discover a whole area of associative rhythm which we have not yet touched on. It is clear that associative speech, if sufficiently confused and off its guard, will often produce the unconscious wit of malapropism, a nice derangement of epitaphs. One step further takes us into the poetic process itself, the largely subconscious free association of words by sound out of which the schemata of poetry develop. In euphuism, where the underlying rhythm is that of prose, such associations are not subconscious but are deliberately added ornament, and this deliberate quality is the reason for the sense of self-parody in euphuism, as though, on Freudian principles, a normally suppressed mental process were made humorous by being openly displayed.

Let us now reverse our direction, starting with a "normal" form of verse, a continuous verse which is equidistant from prose and from an associative rhythm, and see what happens to it as it falls under the influence of a secondary prose rhythm. The heroic couplet is perhaps the clearest example of such normal verse in English. In Pope, for instance, the writing always makes prose sense, but there is no point at which it either leans over toward prose or leans away from it. We hear at once the full ring of the rhyming couplet, and we know immediately what kind of thing to expect. There is a sense of constantly fulfilled expectation, a sense which is the opposite of obviousness. We do not know what Pope is going to say, but we know the units within which he is going to say it. There may be greater poetry than Pope's, but Pope represents, in English, the perfect expression of what is here meant by verse. We also notice in Pope the general principle that the effect of perfected verse, of words moving along in obviously disciplined metrical patterns, is that of epigrammatic wit.

When the rhyme disappears, as it does in blank verse, we take a step nearer to prose, and we find ourselves listening to a syncopated mixture of iambic pentameter and a prose semantic rhythm. The fight of these two rhythms against each other makes up much of the complexity of great blank-verse writing. In some poets, including in their very different ways Milton, Keats and Tennyson, the giving up of rhyme is counterbalanced by an elaborate pattern of assonance. Such a pattern cannot be reduced to a definite scheme like a couplet rhyme, but its presence is clear enough, and so is its absence in most of, say, Wordsworth and

Browning. In the blank verse of these latter poets we find most clearly displayed another secondary or mixed form, verse so strongly affected by prose as to make it often difficult to tell, listening to it read aloud, whether we are listening to verse or to prose. This is the usual rhythmical basis of what is called the conversational style in poetry, a style which is not that of ordinary speech, but a specialized literary imitation of it: *sermoni propriora,* in a Horatian phrase applied by Coleridge to one of his poems. Again, such imitation may approach parody, as it does in the famous pedestrianisms of Wordsworth, e.g., "My drift, I fear, is scarcely obvious"—although this line, which survived all the revisions of the *Prelude,* is a more calculated effect than it looks. In both Wordsworth and Browning there is a revolt against traditional snobbery in poetic language which gives point to an occasional artful sinking. We shall return to this question later. The usefulness of a conversational mixed rhythm for poetic drama is obvious, and in drama, where rhetorical differences between the speeches of different characters is so important, a discontinuous element in the writing becomes functional.

We may now take the next step corresponding to euphuism, where we have a verse pattern as close to prose as it can be and still remain verse: where the prose element in the diction and syntax is so strong that the features of verse still remaining give the effect of continuous parody. This is the area of intentional doggerel, close to what in German is called *knittelvers,* though that term is more specific. Here are the opening lines of Donne's Fourth Satire:

> Well; I may now receive, and die. My sin
> Indeed is great, but yet I have been in
> A purgatory, such as fear'd hell is
> A recreation to and scarce map of this.

No one hearing these lines read aloud would take them for heroic couplet. The rhymes are so weak that they vanish in the reading, and the strong syncopation destroys all suggestion of an iambic meter. We call the result intentional doggerel, because, as in real doggerel, the effective rhythm is prose and the features of rhyme and meter become grotesque. Such doggerel was, by the rules of Renaissance rhetoric, appropriate for satire, and there is no question of Donne's not bothering to write his verse properly. More commonly, however, we find not the disappearing but the obtrusive rhyme, the effect of which is nearly always comic in English. Examples in Butler's *Hudibras*, in Byron's *Don Juan*, in Browning, Gilbert and Ogden Nash come readily to mind. Here again, as with euphuism, we are moving in an atmosphere of parody and paradox, and also of discontinuity. Works of intentional doggerel are usually satires, and digression and constant change of theme and mood are part of the structure of satire. Again we are approaching the creative process, the associative babble out of which poetry comes, but, as with euphuism, are approaching it deliberately and in reverse, as it were. What makes intentional doggerel funny is its implied parody of real doggerel, or incompetent attempts at verse: the struggle for rhymes, even to the mispronouncing of words, the dragging in of ideas for the sake of a rhyme, the distorting of syntax in squeezing words into meter. Again, as in euphuism, a normally subconscious process becomes witty by being transferred to consciousness. Thus Ogden Nash on the cobra:

> This creature fills its mouth with venum
> And walks upon its duodenum.

He who attempts to tease the cobra
Is soon a wiser he, and sobra.

II

WE HAVE now, after examining the influence of
prose and verse rhythms on each other, identified
two common "secondary" rhythms, those of rhetorical prose and of conversational verse, as well
as two more extreme, experimental, or "tertiary"
rhythms, euphuism and satiric doggerel. The two
secondary forms have little in common: verse influenced by prose is quite different in effect from
prose influenced by verse. One of the most striking contrasts is that of speed: the influx of verse
rhythm into prose, which makes prose oratorical,
slows down the speed; the influx of prose into verse,
which makes verse conversational, increases the
speed. The two tertiary forms, on the other hand,
have a good deal in common. We have now to try
to see what forms result when the associative
rhythm influences, or is influenced by, prose and
verse. We shall start with the influence of verse
on a predominantly associative rhythm.

Here we face a new difficulty. The associative

rhythm in itself is sub-literary, and it seldom appears without some kind of verse or prose disguise. In genuinely simple societies there is a communal associative rhythm, of a type that survives in college yells and other crowd chants, and takes the form of simple patterns of repetition, including the device of the catalogue, which is one of the clearest signs of associative influence. Communal associative rhythms are so close to verse that we seldom meet them except after they have crystallized into verse, but incremental repetition and the use of refrains and nonsense words in ballads and folksongs show the associative strain in their ancestry. The nursery rhyme "This is the house that Jack built," and such catalogue songs as "The twelve days of Christmas" are examples of pre-verse association.

But from about 1750 on, literature becomes introspective and sophisticated enough to begin to make more use of the associative rhythm. What is called "free verse" is another secondary or mixed form, an associative rhythm strongly influenced by verse. Free verse is usually a series of phrases with no fixed metrical pattern, the influence of verse being shown in the fact that the phrases are rhythmically separated from one another, not connected by syntax as in prose. Such an associative phrase-rhythm can be heard (with a bit of necessary typographical rearrangement) very clearly in Ossian:

> The wan cold moon rose in the east.
> Sleep descended on the youths.
> Their blue helmets glitter to the beam;
> The fading fire decays.
> But sleep did not rest on the king:
> He rose in the midst of his arms,
> And slowly ascended the hill
> To behold the flame of Sarno's tower.

In free verse the older forms of associative repetition soon reappear: we notice, for example, the fondness of Whitman and other free-verse poets for the catalogue. The free-verse imagists of the nineteen-twenties issued manifestoes saying that poetry should be objective, visual, concentrated, precise, hard, clear and rendering particulars exactly. As with a good deal of poetry written to a theory, the theory was a compensation for the practice: what imagism mainly produced was precisely the opposite, an associative hypnotic chant based on various devices of repetition. John Gould

Fletcher's "color symphonies" are clear examples. In such catalogue poetry as this from Amy Lowell we have perhaps reached the "tertiary" form in this direction, associative writing which is as close to verse as it can be without actually becoming verse:

Lilacs,
False blue,
White,
Purple,
Color of lilac,
Heart-leaves of lilac all over New England,
Roots of lilac under all the soil of New England,
Lilac in me because I am New England . . .

When we come the other way, starting with normal verse and studying the influence of the associative rhythm on it, we are in the more familiar territory of the lyric. We noticed that some poets, including Milton and Keats, if they drop rhyme, remain within the orbit of normal verse by virtue of an indefinable but easily recognized sound-pattern. Such a sound-pattern, however, introduces a slight element of discontinuity, in the form of the "great line." To encounter such a line as "Far into chaos and the world unborn" in *Paradise*

Lost is an invitation to the sensitive reader to stop and meditate, to memorize the line and remember it later in other contexts than those of the poem. Such lines are sibylline or "touchstone" lines. What is more relevant here, their rhythm is a little further from prose and a little closer to the more withdrawn and introspective rhythm of association.

In lyrical poetry, where the normal unit is the stanza, we have a more discontinuous structure, and one which allows of a larger number of the standard poetic devices. Alliteration, inter-rhyming, assonance and refrain can all be added to lyric much more easily than to continuous verse. Lyric, therefore, is another secondary or mixed form, a form of verse, but more strongly influenced by the associative rhythm than continuous verse. Perhaps the clearest way to illustrate its characteristics will be to take the deliberately paradoxical example of Spenser's *Faerie Queene,* where these characteristics appear in the context of an epic. The Spenserian stanza has a most complex rhyme-scheme, and the sense of rhythmical discontinuity that such a stanza provides is emphasized by an Alexandrine at the end, which rounds off each stanza and brings the forward movement to a full stop. Plainly, one is not intended to keep one's finger wet ready to turn the pages of *The Faerie Queene* to see how the story comes out. One is expected to move along meditatively, lost in reverie, responding to the associative element in the alliteration and other patterns of repetition with which Spenser thickens his texture:

> Stout Priamond, but not so strong to strike,
> Strong Diamond, but not so stout a knight,
> But Triamond was stout and strong alike:
> On horseback used Triamond to fight
> And Priamond on foot had more delight,
> But horse and foot knew Diamond to wield:
> With curtaxe used Diamond to smite,
> And Triamond to handle spear and shield,
> But spear and curtaxe both us'd Priamond in field.

Here is a form of verse in which associative patterns are becoming almost obsessive: that is, it brings us near the limit of associative influence on verse, to an extreme or "tertiary" mixed form like those of euphuism, intentional doggerel, and Amy Lowell's rhapsodic rhythm. There is no name for this form: perhaps we could call it echolalia. Echolalia in Spenser is particularly effective for temptation scenes, like those of Acrasia and Despair: a very clear example is this five-part madrigal in the description of the Bower of Bliss, the five parts being named in the Alexandrine of the previous stanza: "Birds, voices, instruments, winds, waters, all agree":

> The joyous birds shrouded in cheerful shade,
>> Their notes unto the voice attempered sweet;
>> Th' angelical soft trembling voices made
>> To th' instruments divine respondence meet:
>> The silver sounding instruments did meet
>> With the bass murmur of the water's fall:
>> The waters fall with difference discreet,
>> Now soft, now loud, unto the wind did call:
> The gentle warbling wind low answered to all.

A stanza of a similar type (II, iv, 35) was quoted in a contemporary rhetoric book before *The Faerie Queene* itself was published. The purpose of a deliberate rhetorical exercise in such a scene is not simply to cast a spell but to suggest the paradox of something which does cast a spell and yet remains evil.

We notice the identical rhyme "meet" in the above stanza, probably the only word in the language that would have been meet for such a purpose. Identical rhymes usually give the effect of a clashing or blurring of sound, and we find similar blurrings in the drowsy narcotic scenes in Spenser which mark the assimilation of the stanzaic epic to the dreamy romance. The assonance of "noise" and "annoy" is as correct in the description of the cave of Morpheus as it would be incorrect elsewhere:

> No other noise, nor peoples' troublous cries,
> As still are wont t'annoy the walled town
> Might there be heard . . .

It is a general principle of rhetoric that dream states are expressed by intensified sound-patterns, as in *Pearl* or *Kubla Khan*. In other poets too we find repetitions of sound that would simply be blemishes in a less associative type of verse but are in order when we are close to reverie, as in Collins' *Ode to Evening:*

> With brede ethereal *wove*
> O'erhang his *wavy* bed

or in the last line of Keats's *Ode to Melancholy:*

> And be *among* her cloudy trophies *hung*.

Dream poetry has a curious bifocal quality to it: the ingenuity involved in its elaborations is like the ingenuity of the dream itself. It seems charming, in the original sense of the word, as long as we are bound by its spell, but when we escape from that spell into full consciousness we see the elaboration as witty ingenuity. Thus in Poe, who naturally comes to mind when we think of associative poetry, we find rhetorical devices so obtrusive that it is difficult not to analyze them in detail, as Poe did himself. Once, again, as with euphuism and satiric doggerel, we are in a world of discontinuity, paradox and verbal wit. Poe's critical theory is a theory of the essential discontinuity of all poetry: *The Bells* and *The Raven* are dreamlike poems which are yet close to light verse, and the line from *The City in the Sea,* "The viol, the violet, and the vine," is pure *Finnegans Wake* punning. Ernest Dowson is said to have called this line the ideal of a line of verse, which is probably correct. That is, to be looking for the ideal line in whatever language shows a strongly associative tendency, which only a line as associative as this is likely to satisfy. Similarly with Swinburne:

> We shift and bedeck and bedrape us,
>   Thou art noble and nude and antique;

Libitina thy mother, Priapus
   Thy father, a Tuscan and Greek.
We play with light loves in the portal,
   And wince and relent and refrain;
Loves die, and we know thee immortal,
   Our Lady of Pain.

This is not exactly satiric doggerel, for the context is solemn, and it is not incompetent doggerel, for Swinburne is too competent a poet. Like Poe's *The Bells* and *The Raven*, it is dreamlike and witty at once, a kind of verbal blues or pensive jazz.

Echolalia is common in religious verse, for a reason that will not surprise us by now: repetition of sound increases the sense of meditation, or concentrating the mind on a single object or idea. Here the two states of dreaming and waking consciousness focus into one, the state of vision, or its auditory equivalent. In Donne, Herbert, Hopkins, and Eliot, we find moods which express intense religious emotion through paradoxical wit, which latter seems a part of the emotion and not something "yoked by violence," in Johnson's phrase, to it. Examples are familiar: there are Donne's intricate conceits about the dying of death and the corners of the round earth, Herbert's visual conceits of poems in the shape of altars or wings, and a curious tendency to jingle and sound-clash, ranging from Donne's pun on his own name, "When thou hast done, thou hast not done," to such phrases as "it tosses up our losses," or "words, after speech, reach" in Eliot's *Quartets*. A more elaborate example, Hopkins' "Jack, joke, poor potsherd, patch, matchwood, immortal diamond," associates the paradoxes of incarnation and redemption with (among half a dozen other allusions) the identity of substance in matchwood and diamond, the incongruity of which is further emphasized by the sound-clashes. Such simultaneous use of reverence and joke in religious verse goes back to the puns of the Old Testament and the ambivalence of the ancient oracles.

Associative rhythms move toward prose in much the same way that they move toward verse. Criticism does not appear to have any such term as "free prose" to describe an associative rhythm influenced, but not quite organized, by the sentence. But that free prose exists is clear enough, and in fact it develops much earlier than free verse. We find some free prose in personal letters, where the tendency to associative monologue is so strong that convention has had to devise a great number of ways for getting a letter stopped. We must close now and do something else; we are in good health and hope you are the same; and we finally reach yours sincerely like a liner being towed into port. But the letter is still a form of communication, and free prose is more obvious in diaries, especially diaries kept by people of no great literary pretensions who are not thinking of publication. The seventeenth-century Yankee Samuel Sewall kept a diary of this sort, and it is easy to see not only an associative style but an associative habit of mind as, on a voyage across the Atlantic, he records random impressions one after another, not in the more causal sequence that prose would demand:

Tuesday Nov. 27, sail East-South-East, and sometimes East and North. Ait my wives Pastry, the remembrance of whom is ready to cut me to the heart. The Lord pardon and help me . . . Friday, Dec. 7th, very fair day: sail N. East. Breakfast on one of my wives Plum Cakes. Read Dr. Preston Saints Support of sorrowful Sinners. One of the Geese dyes yesterday, or to day. Mrs. Baxter is better . . .

In literature free prose is particularly congenial to prose satire, with its disintegrating approach to form and logical connection. We find it in Rabelais, and even Swift, at the very summit of English prose, seems to collapse with relief into the associative baby talk of the *Journal to Stella*. Burton's *Anatomy of Melancholy* is a tremendous masterpiece of free prose, where quotations, references, allusions, titles of books, Latin tags, short sharp phrases, long lists and catalogues, are all swept up in one vast exuberant associative wave. In Sterne's *Tristram Shandy*, where nuances of gesture and posture are as important as the dialogue, the quick darting rhythm is intensely associative. When Corporal Trim is inspired to a speech on mortality, the style is anything but oratorical, for Sterne has too many other things to watch:

Are we not, continued Trim, looking still at Susannah—are we not like a flower of the field—a tear of pride stole in betwixt every two tears of humiliation —else no tongue could have described Susannah's affliction—is not all flesh grass?—'Tis clay,—'tis dirt. —They all looked directly at the scullion,—the scullion had just been scouring a fish-kettle.—It was not fair.—

—What is the finest face that ever man looked at! —I could hear Trim talk so for ever, cried Susannah,—what is it! (Susannah laid her hand upon

Trim's shoulder)—but corruption?—Susannah took it off.

A glance at Sterne's expressive punctuation and his almost continuous use of the dash, which he puts even with a period, shows that the rhythmical unit of his writing is not the sentence. In free prose the punctuation is the main clue to the speed at which the associative process is assumed to be travelling. The slow-moving meditations of Bloom in *Ulysses* are punctuated by periods; Sterne, and Jingle in Dickens, rely on the dash; Burton, still faster, uses mainly the comma, and the uninhibited rush through the mind of Molly Bloom at the end of *Ulysses* has no punctuation at all, giving the whole book the musical feature of a presto finale. After Sterne, whose revolution in prose was comparable to that of his contemporary Ossian in verse, associative and prose rhythms mingle in fiction, particularly in "stream-of-consciousness" fiction, where either rhythm may take the lead. We also have more extreme forms of free prose, with echolalia and repetition of sound and of thematic words, of a kind, again, often appropriate to a religious setting. Prayer in particular, where the writer is turning his back on his audience, and where his state of mind is one of fixed concentration, often develops such extreme forms. Thus from Donne's *Meditations:*

. . . thou callest Gennezareth, which was but a Lake, and not salt, a Sea; so thou callest the Mediterranean Sea, still the great Sea, because the inhabitants saw no other Sea; they that dwelt there, thought a Lake, a Sea, and the others thought a little Sea, the greatest . . .

Let us now return to normal prose and study the associative influence on it. We began this survey with a passage of formal or "written" prose standing at some distance from the associative rhythm. In such prose as Darwin's the sentence rhythm is very clear, to the point of being obtrusive. Here, in contrast, is a passage from Bernard Shaw:

After all, what man is capable of the insane self-conceit of believing that an eternity of himself would be tolerable even to himself? Those who try to believe it postulate that they shall be made perfect first. But if you make me perfect I shall no longer be myself, nor will it be possible for me to conceive my present imperfections (and what I cannot conceive I cannot remember); so that you may just as well give me a new name and face the fact that I am a new person and that the old Bernard Shaw is as dead as mutton.

We notice the tone of ordinary conversation with the reader, the easy use of parenthesis, the unforced repetition of certain words and ideas. All these are features of associative writing, and hence bring the prose closer to normal articulate speech.

A piece of continuous prose, whatever its tone, looks at first sight like a dictatorial form, in which there is a one-sided and undisturbed monologue proceeding from the author. Looking more carefully, however, we can see that in adopting an expository form the author is really putting himself on a level with his reader, with whom the continuity of his rhythm keeps him in a point-for-point relation. If a writer wishes to suggest a kind of aloofness; if he wishes to suggest that it is the reader's business to come to him and not his business to come to the reader; if he wishes to suggest that there are riches in his mind which his actual writing gives no more than a hint of, he will have to adopt a different kind of prose style. Such a style would be discontinuous, breaking up a straightforward exposition into a sequence of aphorisms, usually with typographical breaks in between.

The use of discontinuous aphorisms suggests to the reader that here is something he must stop and meditate on, aphorism by aphorism, that he must enter into the writer's mind instead of merely following his discourse. What one says is surrounded by silence, as though a hidden context of mental activity lay behind every formulated sentence. And here, at last, the more technical and stylistic problems of this chapter begin to connect with the social and educational problems of the previous one.

This discontinuous aphoristic style has been in all ages and cultures the standard rhetoric of wisdom. There are different levels of it, just as there are different levels of wisdom, and on the upper levels we can see the lower ones as relatively commonplace. Perhaps we should reverse the words upper and lower, because the usual metaphors contrast the deep with the shallow, the profound with the superficial. On the shallowest levels we find clichés, formulations that may once have represented mental activity but are now only substitutes for it, automatic responses that give those who are not thinking the illusion of thought. Next come the accepted ideas, the Bouvard-and-

Pécuchet instinct to be justified by faith in rumor. Next are the proverbs which express the inherited wisdom of simple and therefore deeply conservative societies. Proverbs have been central to verbal culture since the days of ancient Egypt, and, as we can see from the proverbial books of the Old Testament, they revolve around a conception of wisdom as the tried and tested way of behavior, in contrast to the folly which seizes on an old fallacy as a new discovery. Proverbial philosophy is closer to literature than to actual philosophy, because the poet or literary artist seeks, not the unexplored idea, but the inevitable expression of the familiar idea.

The difference in level between shallow platitude and profound aphorism makes for a good deal of parody in this region of literature. Modern wit would be considerably impoverished if it did not have clichés and accepted ideas to make fun of or reverse. Any comedy of Oscar Wilde will furnish a great number of such inverted clichés, and, on a more intense imaginative plane, Blake's Proverbs of Hell are parodied reversals of popular commonplaces of the "nothing in excess" or "you travel most safely by the middle road" variety.

This feature of parodied commonplace may be very old: the real form of the Book of Ecclesiastes in the Bible appears to be a collection of stock proverbs subjected to analysis in the light of the author's conception of the real meaning of wisdom as the ability to see through "vanity." The particular type of aphorism we call the epigram is characterized by a wit which operates by oversimplifying its subject, usually by assimilating it to some grammatical feature of expression, such as analogy or antithesis or pun. In Emerson's comment on critics, "The borer on our peach trees bores that she may deposit an egg: but the borer into theories and institutions and books bores that he may bore," it is pun. In Shaw's "The conversion of a savage to Christianity is the conversion of Christianity to savagery," it is antithesis. In Blake's "Prudence is a rich, ugly old maid courted by Incapacity," it is analogy.

Naturally philosophers themselves, being lovers of wisdom, are much attached to the discontinuous aphoristic form. Not only did Western philosophy itself grow out of the aphoristic forms used by the great pre-Socratics, but the tradition continues at least in Bacon and Spinoza, and in our day in

Wittgenstein. Here the more purely philosophical concern shows itself in the attention given to sequence and logical progression. The literary interest tends to detach the aphorism from its context. Humanistic education ransacked the great writers for *sententiae* or *adagia,* profound, witty or inspiring comments on the human situation. The sententious approach to literature is still the popular one, accounting for the wide appeal of such poems as Kipling's *If* or Longfellow's *Psalm of Life,* and even the cultivated man's ability to frame his own conceptions is regularly accompanied by the ability to quote, to find parallel expressions in his cultural heritage.

The proverb is a counsel of action, and popular proverbs are normally counsels of prudent action, designed for those who are without great advantages of birth or wealth, and so need signposts indicating the safest roads. But the connection of the proverb with action, the fact that in it *quid credas* is also *quid agas,* makes the aphoristic style the inevitable form of rhetoric for religion also. It is the appropriate form for the sermons of religious teachers, including Jesus and Buddha, of whom it seems for some reason significant to say that they do not write. Here the aphorisms are related to a total vision of life (*quo tendas*) and so become more than pragmatically moral. As the philosopher's bent is revealed in the importance he attaches to sequence and logical progression when he uses aphorisms, so the religious bent is existential. The aphorisms are formulated at certain times of the teacher's life, to answer a question, to comment on an incident, to articulate a moment of significance.

In modern literature, an important by-product of the aphoristic tradition is a form of oracular writing which for some reason is more common in French and German literature than in English, represented by, among others, Paul Fort, St. John Perse, René Char, and Rimbaud's *Saison en Enfer*. This is classified, no doubt rightly, as poetry, but its rhythmical basis is an aphoristic and associative form of prose. The use of prose rather than verse as the rhythmical basis for such writing as the *Saison en Enfer* has an inherently paradoxical quality in it which indicates that it is one of our "tertiary" forms. Just as extreme realism or *trompe l'oeil* in painting seems to acquire, when pursued far enough, the unnatural glittering clarity of hallucination, so it is prose, the rhythm of ordinary consciousness, which provides the corresponding quality in literature. The closely related *Also Sprach Zarathustra* shows the connection of the literary form with religious and prophetic rhetoric.

The more extreme and experimental aphoristic prose becomes, the more elusive and paradoxical the meaning. We finally reach a point at which the associative influence is so strong that the appearance of prose has an effect of parody similar to what we noticed in other tertiary forms. One of René Char's aphorisms, for instance, is simply "Devoirs infernaux," though the English translation, "What I have to do is hell," rescues it for prose. Here we are close to the koan of Zen Buddhism or the mantra of Hinduism, where a baffling and paradoxical verbal formula is proposed as a subject for meditation. Such techniques have for their object the attempt to break down or through the whole structure of verbal articulation, and we are reminded of Rimbaud's "dérèglement de tous les sens." But usually with poets such enigmatic phrases seem to have some connection with the creative process. Yeats is a good example: Mallarmé's phrase about the trembling of the veil of the temple and the oracle that emerges from the darkness of *Axël* about our servants doing our living for us have sent many a critic off on a quite mistaken quest for the "influence" of Mallarmé and *Axël* on Yeats.

III

WE HAVE distinguished the problems of ordinary speech from those of literature, but the same distinction creates a difference of emphasis in literature itself. Poets have always disagreed about the relation of literature to ordinary speech. One view, represented in our day by Valéry, is that literature as compared with music is under a great disadvantage in not having a separate verbal language. The sounds of violins and pianos are in a different world from the sounds of ordinary life, but the poet, using the same words that everyone else uses, is in the position of a composer who has to make his symphony out of street noises. Hence, for Valéry, what is usually called poetic diction has a functional role in literature, as it attempts to set up a language within a language which is especially designed for poetry. The opposite tendency is represented by Wordsworth's familiar preface, where we are told that poetry should avoid all special diction and employ the language really used by men.

These two tendencies in literature we may call the hieratic and the demotic. The hieratic tendency seeks out formal elaborations of verse and prose. The hieratic poet finds, with Valéry, that the kind of poetry he wants to write depends, like chess, on complex and arbitrary rules, and he experiments with patterns of rhythm, rhyme and assonance, as well as with mythological and other forms of specifically poetic imagery. The demotic tendency is to minimize the difference between literature and speech, to seek out the associative or prose rhythms that are used in speech and reproduce them in literature. With this distinction in mind, let us sum up what we have said about literary rhythms and go back to the problem we were led to in the last chapter, the problem of what is meant by the traditional distinction of low, middle and high styles. This time we are approaching the question as a technical problem in literary criticism, though we have given reasons for thinking that it is of considerably more than technical importance.

In demotic literature the "low" style is, in general, the literary use of colloquial and familiar speech. Wordsworth's preface, with its references to humble and rustic life, emphasizes the affinity of his style with certain social classes, and expresses a defiance of the traditional snobbery which on social grounds instinctively says, with the cronies of Tony Lumpkin, "Damn anything that's low." Coleridge's famous criticism of Wordsworth supplies a link essential to our argument but missing in Wordsworth's, that ordinary speech is one thing and the literary use of it another. The moral considerations advanced in the previous chapter about the use of associative rhythms in ordinary speech clearly have no relevance to a deliberate and conscious employment of such rhythms for literary purposes. Wordsworth's approach to low style is normally connected with his literary development of ballad and broadside conventions. When he is writing in his own person, as in *The Prelude*, he keeps as a rule to middle style. In some writers the use of middle style freezes into a rigid decorum, where passages for which a familiar or colloquial language would be appropriate seem to pose a kind of dilemma, with the writer having to choose between euphemism and bathos. Even Wordsworth runs into this difficulty occasionally in *The Excursion*.

In a good deal of fiction and drama, especially in the nineteenth century, the difference between genteel and vulgar idiom, or between low-style dialogue and the author's middle-style narrative and description, may be so sharp as to divide the work into different languages. Whitman's *Song of Myself* is an example of a work which is theoretically in low style, but is actually in middle style with a number of deliberate colloquialisms inserted to provide a lower tone. At other times the author may assimilate his own style to that of internal characters, as Hemingway does; or, as in *Huckleberry Finn*, tell a story through the spoken idiom of one character; or, as on the famous opening page of *A Sentimental Journey*, take or pretend to take the reader at once into his intimate personal life. Low demotic style is also found in intentional doggerel, from *Hudibras* to *Sweeney Agonistes*.

One very sophisticated and difficult form of

low demotic has a particular relevance to our present argument. This is the attempt in fiction to isolate and catch the steady stream of querulous, neurotic, compulsive babble coming from what we have called the ego, that is, a consciousness imprisoned in the restrictive self, and which, being conscious, knows that it is imprisoned. The voice of this ego is first heard, to my knowledge (so far as anything can be first in literature), in the book of Dostoievsky whose title is usually translated as *Notes from Underground*. A fine contemporary expression of it is Samuel Beckett's trilogy, known in English as *Molloy, Malone Dies* and *The Unnamable*. As the voice of the ego is the voice of tedium itself, it is something of a *tour de force* to make it interesting to a reader, and so it is usually presented indirectly or in symbol. In Forster's *A Passage to India,* for instance, it is symbolized by the echo in the Marabar caves, described as "Something very old and very small . . . Something snub-nosed, incapable of generosity—the undying worm itself—the serpent of eternity made of maggots."

Low hieratic style, on the other hand, takes us into the area of creative association, the babble of echoing sounds out of which poetry eventually comes, and which are reproduced, sometimes with deliberate or conscious wit, in the experimental or "tertiary" forms we have been discussing: euphuism, echolalia and the like. In prose satire, from Rabelais on, we often meet associative passages in macaronic or other experimental forms of language. Here again, as with low demotic, the author may employ the style himself or represent it dramatically through characters. It is rare to find, at least before the twentieth century, an author employing it himself, except in very special cases, Smart's *Jubilate Agno* being one of the most notable in English. The greatest dramatic example of it is certainly *Finnegans Wake*, an extraordinary monument of associative writing, and a kind of encyclopedia of experimental styles.

"Low" style, we see, does have about it, on its demotic side, some of its traditional associations with the speech of uneducated or inarticulate people. But if the term is to be of any real use in criticism, we have to think of "low" style as concerned primarily with words in process, language which for one reason or another deliberately falls short of or by-passes conventionally articulate communication. It is heavily influenced by the associative rhythm because, as we saw in the previous chapter, the associative rhythm represents the process of bringing ideas into articulation, in contrast to prose or verse, which normally represent a finished product. Low style is also the area of free verse and free prose, where we consent to a suspending of conventional rules in order to gain the advantages of experiment, verisimilitude, or a deeper exploration of society or the writer's mind. Without it, literature would tend to become identified with conventional rhetorics.

Middle demotic style needs no comment: what is meant by it here, the ordinary language of communication which is at once plain and cultivated, should be clear enough by now. Its normal medium is expository prose or narrative or didactic verse. Middle hieratic is the ordinary formal language of poetic expression. Much of it consists of what Hopkins, in one of his brilliant early letters, calls "Parnassian"—the consciously literary style that a poet develops and gets to use out of habit. Such a style may go wrong in trying to deal with familiar or commonplace events for which a demotic style would be more appropriate, as in the description of fish-selling in Tennyson's *Enoch Arden* that was noted by Bagehot as over-ornate. This is one of the occupational hazards of hieratic style, and one that we are sensitive to in this demotic age, just as earlier ages were sensitive to the low or "mean." Deliberately rhetorical prose, of the type already discussed, belongs here too. Middle style represents literature as an art of conventional communication, so that its rhetoric tends to become either habitual or transparent, or both, and it expresses itself primarily in a sense of structure. For structure is what our attention is focussed on as soon as we become accustomed to a style or do not notice it.

Perhaps the most concentrated of all middle-style techniques is that represented by the formulaic epic and its development in the Homeric poems. Blake once suggested that there were no epigrams in Homer: this may be an over-statement, but it is true that in Homer expression is subordinated to theme and structure to a degree unapproached in more self-conscious literature. The combining and recombining of conventional metrical units makes possible a repetitive intensity that in modern art can be matched only in certain qualities of music. The last line of the *Iliad:* "Thus they buried Hector, tamer of horses," is one of the most deeply impressive lines in literature, simply because it is the last line of the *Iliad.* The units out of which it is constructed are epic commonplaces, just as the last measure of a Mozart or Beethoven symphony might be a simple perfect cadence, identical with the last measure of nothing by nobody.

As we listen to demotic language, we are constantly, if unconsciously, making judgements along a certain scale of impression. At the bottom of the scale we have: this is commonplace; everybody knows that; we've heard it all before. Next come: this logically follows; yes, I see that. Occasionally, however, something emerges that seems to have a magic circle drawn around it, expressing something in us as well as in itself, which halts the progress of an argument and demands meditation. Whenever we have this feeling we are, or think we are, in the presence of high demotic style. Here we have reached the pinnacle of the ladder of *sententiae* which we discussed a few pages back.

For high demotic style is essentially aphoristic, whether it is in verse or prose. It deals, almost necessarily, with the traditional and the familiar, and with those moments of response to what we feel most deeply in ourselves, whether love, loyalty or reverence. There is thus an ethical factor in high demotic style which the term "sublime" expresses. Such points of concentration do not differ in kind from middle or low style, and hence do not violate the context from which they emerge. They are of relatively short duration, as they do not depend on sequence or connection. What they do depend on is the active participation of the reader or hearer: they are points which the reader recognizes as appropriate for the focussing of his own consciousness. They are moments when the normal detachment that separates reader from writer gives way to the reader's feeling that he has not simply understood the writer, but has entered into some kind of common ground or order with him. Questions of how the simplicity of high style differs from commonplace, of how the genuine differs from the pinchbeck, of what obligation it is that compels our active participation, and the like, have been discussed at least since Longinus.

High style is essentially discontinuous, and nothing is written throughout in high demotic style except sacred writings, which owe their continuous height to social acceptance. Such acceptance expands the random remarks and local allusions of the original into statements of universal significance. Because of social acceptance, Paul's views on the headgear of women in Corinth or the method of appointing elders in Galatia have acquired a tremendous resonance in Christian churches, and the disagreements of Engels and Dühring, or Lenin's advice on the tactics of a strike, have gained a similar universally authoritative quality in Communist countries. The literary form of religious revelation, such as the Mosaic law or the Koran, is also discontinuous, breaking down into specific commandments or illustrations. In the Christian gospel, where a divine personality is presented, the only possible literary form would be that of a discontinuous sequence of epiphanies, which is the form that modern critics have discovered in it.

For high hieratic style, a somewhat cacophonous term to which I seem to be committed, some more modern word like "intensity" is better than sublimity. We have high style in this mode when we feel the sense of what Joyce calls epiphany in a secular and specifically literary context, a momentary coordination of vision, a passage which stands out from its context demanding to be not merely read but possessed. The emphasis here is more individual than social, and the ethical element in the response less important. The lyric attempts to isolate this kind of intensity; in a longer poem certain passages stand out with a distinctive kind of luminousness, to which Horace's abominable phrase "purple patch" hardly does justice. It was Poe who recognized the affinity of the lyric and the intense passages in longer poems, and suggested that the middle-style construction out of which these passages emerged was really sub-poetic.

Several modern poets have followed up this suggestion, and Eliot, Pound, Valéry, Rilke and others write discontinuous poems in which everything that must be said, in Valéry's phrase, has been eliminated. The continuity, in effect, has been handed over to the reader. This technique gives to such fragmented and discontinuous poetry an oracular quality, corresponding closely to the aphoristic style of high demotic. In the Eliot *Quartets,* however, we notice that brief passages of lyrical intensity alternate with passages written in a deliberately prosaic and middle-style rhetoric. This reminds us of a more traditional method of stressing the emotional contrast between intensity and continuity—the method of writing a series of lyrics or parts of lyrics connected by prose narrative or commentary, employed by two poets who have profoundly influenced Eliot: Dante in the *Vita Nuova,* and St. John of the Cross in *The Dark Night of the Soul.* The poetry in the latter work is related to the Song of Songs in the Bible, and derives much of its authoritative tone from its predecessor. Works based on an interconnection of oracular poetry and prose commentary are usually found in or near the area of religion (even Madame Blavatsky's *Secret Doctrine* takes this form).

Poe's theory that a long poem is a contradiction, to which we have just referred, is an attempt to define high style in purely hieratic terms. He separates poetry as sharply as possible from other verbal structures, recognizes the discontinuity of high style, and finds its basis in feeling alone, as everything we have associated with high demotic style has for him to be ruled out of poetry. Our present argument seems to indicate the existence of two kinds of "high" literary experience, one demotic and one hieratic, one in general verbal practice and one more strictly confined to literature; one a recognition of something like verbal truth and the other a recognition of something like verbal beauty. High style in demotic writing depends largely on social acceptance: it is the apotheosis of the proverb, the axioms that a society takes to its business and bosom. Hieratic writing is more dependent on canons of taste and esthetic judgement, admittedly more flexible and more elusive than counsels of behavior. For the genuine and sincere writer, everything he writes is in high style: he means every line with the maximum of intensity, and is apt to become exasperated with readers whose reception of his work is tepid or selective. In an art of communication, however, social acceptance is still necessary to make such intensity permanent. The development of a community of taste is slower and more haphazard than the development of a community of behavior, but it still takes place. Arnold's "touchstones" of high style are subjectively intuited and their merit is indemonstrable, like all critical value-judgements, but still a community can respond to them, can feel that Arnold's taste, within obvious limits, is accurate and that his quotations are accurate.

The example of Homer, given a few pages back, suggests that Poe's theory, however useful as a guide to a certain kind of technique, is inadequate as an observation on literature in general. The theory implies that a "great" long poem is a poem in which great passages tear themselves loose from their context. We notice that of Arnold's touchstones, some are demotic, some hieratic, and some, like the passage from the *Chanson de Roland,* are representative of a certain level of writing. This last is a feature of Arnold's theory which makes it more complete than Poe's. The touchstone passage may also be related to a context, and in its context, the touchstone guarantees that the whole work in which it occurs is worth our attention. In fact a line may be a "touchstone" and yet worthless or unintelligible apart from its context, the stock example being "Never, never, never, never, never" from *King Lear.* The implication is that the authority of high style depends in part on the unity of the work in which it is to be found. No brilliant passage carries real author-ity unless it seems, in the long run, to emerge in-evitably from its context.

But if high style demands a context, the entire work in which it occurs has its context too. The passage in high style is not simply a recognition of truth or beauty in verbal form: it is also a kind of recognition scene in the reader's verbal experi-ence. What implications this has for the theory of criticism we shall try to discuss next.

3. All Ye Know on Earth

LITERARY criticism is more complicated than most disciplines. As a rule we begin with a student and what he studies, confronting each other in a relation of subject and object. But criticism presents us first of all with a triangle. A subject and an object, a group of people called writers and a class of things called in the aggregate literature, are being studied from a third position by people like us. People like us form the audience or public which is the final cause of literature, if there is such a thing: the total body of social response which every writer assumes by the act of writing. It is theoretically possible to write to please oneself without thought of an audience. What is not possible is that such work should be distinguishable, in its conventions and genres, from that of other writers who please to live or instruct to preserve their self-respect. I can think of one author who asserted that his book was a private dream written out merely to gratify himself, but this was Bunyan speaking of *The Pilgrim's Progress,* not usually regarded as an example of pure self-expression. Not only is it didactic and allegorical, but its typed characters, Talkative, Brisk, By-Ends, have much more in common with the Fopling Flutters and Tunbelly Clumsies of contemporary comedy than Bunyan would ever have admitted or realized.

At present we shall represent the literary public by a single sympathetic and informed person, whom we shall call the critic. The critic, then, is exposed to a series of impressions from literature, and by responding to these as carefully as possible, he develops, by practice, a skill and flexibility, for which the traditional term in English is taste. Taste, when acquired, may in turn lead to general theories about the process or products of literature, if general theory happens to be the bent of a critic's interest. The impact of literature on a critic, and the critic's responses to it, make up an area of criticism that is best called rhetorical. Rhetorical criticism in this sense is concerned with the "effects" of literature: it is in other words practical criticism. Reversing the direction of this flow of literature toward the critic gives us the conception of the study of literature as organized by a theory of criticism, which is what is usually meant by poetics.

A critic may have precise and candid taste and yet be largely innocent of theory. Charles Lamb was such a critic, and one feels even that his lack of theory was an advantage to him. Coleridge, on the contrary, was one of the greatest of critical theorists, and yet had much less of Lamb's ability to respond directly to poetry without being confused by moral, religious and political anxieties. But theory, even when the theorist has a shaky practical foundation, is still essential to criticism, for it is only theory that can define, or outline, its specific subject. Aristotle, who founded poetics, wrote a separate treatise on rhetoric, a treatise concerned more with lawcourts and objective truth than with literature; yet he recognized the overlapping of the two areas, and in the *Poetics* sets aside certain critical problems as belonging to rhetoric. But the *Poetics* as a whole separates the area of literature (or "poetry") from other forms of verbal expression. Rhetoric alone cannot do this. In rhetoric all the problems of discursive writing—the author's intention, the direct appeal to the reader, moral value, evidence and truth— get mixed up with literary problems. From the lectures of the sophist to the textbooks of the sophomore, rhetoric has dealt not solely with literature but with "effective communication" in words as a whole.

If we keep our figure of the triangle in mind, we can see that there are two aspects of literary rhetoric: oratory, or the persuasion of an audience, and ornament, or the figuring of speech. This distinction is the basis of the one we made earlier between demotic and hieratic literature. There are two corresponding aspects of poetic theory, related to a common context usually identified with nature. These two emphases are often referred to by the terms Romantic and Classical.

The Classical emphasis, established in Aristotle, is esthetic ("hieratic") in the sense that it is focussed on the thing made, and assumes an emotional balance or detachment which we see in such aspects of it as catharsis. The fundamental conception of this approach is that of "imitation," which is concerned with the relation of the poem to its context in nature. The other emphasis goes back to Plato, but its chief ancient spokesman is Longinus, whose interest in the personal relation of author and hearer and in the category of experience he calls the "sublime" has run through all its history. This emphasis is psychological rather than esthetic, and is based on participation rather than on detachment. It thinks of a poem as an "expression," to use Croce's term, rather than as Aristotle's *techne* or artifact, and its fundamental conception, corresponding to "imitation," is "creation," a metaphor which relates the poet to his context in nature.

The two conceptions of "nature" differ correspondingly. The mimetic tradition thinks of the poem in a context of physical nature, of which we are, to some degree, spectators. It thinks of nature as a structure or system into which the poem fits by "imitation," however imitation is conceived. The creative tradition tends to think of nature as a total creative process of which the poet's creation forms part. The mimetic tradition uses metaphors of objective order; the creative tradition uses metaphors of organism and genesis. Most critics between Ben Jonson and Samuel Johnson are on the mimetic side, and speak of nature as an external model for the poet to "follow." Romantic critics speak very differently. "Believe me," says Coleridge, "you must master the essence, the *natura naturans*, which presupposes a bond between nature in the higher sense and the soul of man." Or, as Shelley seems to come close to saying, trees may be made by any fool of a demiurge, but only God, if there is a God, can make a poem.

The mimetic tradition, stressing as it does the detachment of the work of art from the person who contemplates it, can hardly avoid expressing itself in figures of eyesight and space. The tag *ut pictura poesis* runs all through mimetic criticism, with its overtones of a controlled hallucination. In the poetry and criticism of the last century, metaphors of vision in daylight were carried to extraordinary lengths: in Rimbaud's doctrine that the poet is to *se faire voyant* and produce the *illumination;* in later theories of "imagism"; in the conception of poetic objectivity in Eliot, which is closely linked with the "clear visual images" he ascribes to Dante. The creative tradition, though often attracted toward the same language, makes more use of aural and temporal metaphors, stresses the importance of the speaking voice and the evocative quality of rhythm and sound, and has more tolerance for the sense of mystery, obscurity and magic, for unexplored resources of meaning, and other synonyms for hearing in the dark.

The mimetic tradition, in short, stresses the product in which the completed form of the chicken is prior to the egg; for the creative tradition, being interested in process, the priority of the egg is what is obvious. In all such arguments a fair hearing should be granted to both sides, since in the meantime both chicken and egg exist. Our best critical models from this point of view are eclectic ones, like the Elizabethans who put statements about imitation derived at third hand from Aristotle directly beside statements about creation derived at about fifth hand from Plato.

Or the eighteenth-century critics who paired off the "sublime," the sense of something greater than ourselves that we feel impelled to participate in, with the "beautiful," the more limited and manageable object that can be studied with less sense of involvement. The critic, therefore, is confronted with an odd mixture of participation and detachment, which seem equally important, yet hard to reconcile with each other.

If we think of the poem as an imitation of nature, we can see that a work of art splits nature in two by imitating it. If a landscape painter is "imitating" a real landscape, he imitates a part of nature which remains outside the picture. Nature in this sense is the environment of art, and its position as an environment is the source of all such metaphors as "holding the mirror up to nature." Nature as environment in space is also, in time, the area of the artist's individual experience. In this context nature is the external occasion of the work of art. It provides the nightingales that Keats heard before he wrote his ode, the sexual experiences that Donne had before his *Songs and Sonnets,* and such events as the drowning of Edward King which was the occasion of *Lycidas.* In literature nature as environment plays an essential, though usually minor, role in the creative process.

There remains the question of the landscape as imitated within the picture. Here nature is the content or material cause of the picture. Content is something to be contained, hence nature, conceived as the content of art, is inside art. The form of a painted landscape is a pictorial form. It has a relation to the landscape outside, but the landscape outside is not the source of its form. If it were, the painter would be trying to compete with nature on nature's own ground, or else he would be trying to give us a smudged and oily substitute for a real landscape, designed perhaps to call it up in our memories. This is the Socratic paradox at the end of the *Republic*, and there is no avoiding its conclusion that if art is a second-hand copy of external nature, it has no point or place in civilized human life.

If, now, we think of the poem as a poet's creation, we can see that the act of creation also splits the poet's personality in two. Poets themselves have constantly told us that they do not think of themselves as autonomous shapers of their poems;

that their ordinary personalities are really ob-
servers of a largely involuntary process. Hence the
number of metaphors of relaxed will that we find
poets using: Wordsworth's recollection in tran-
quillity, Keats's negative capability, Eliot's cata-
lyzer image, and the traditional appeal to a Muse
who is supposed to do the actual creative work.
In this century the distinction has sometimes been
given in deliberately paradoxical forms, such as
Yeats's conception of the poetic personality as a
"mask" or compensation for the ordinary one,
Joyce's indifferent god, or Eliot's theory of the
poetic process as "impersonal." Poetry is not
strictly impersonal, but in many respects it is less
misleading to think of it as such than to think of
it as produced by some "hero as poet," an im-
posing personality of which poetry is the direct
expression.

We notice how critics in all ages have preferred
simplicity to cleverness in a poet. As early as
Longinus we have the remark that it is the test
of a good figure of speech when the fact that it
is a figure goes unrecognized. The good writer is
similarly assumed to have a virtue which is esthetic and ethical at once, of being able to keep

out of his work anything which does not "belong,"
however striking or brilliant it may be in itself.
Johnson attacks "metaphysical" poetry because
for him it does not exhibit this virtue. Coleridge's
distinction of imagination and fancy is in part a
distinction between complete integrity and integrity broken by ingenuity, and here again, as in
Johnson, the example of the inferior type is
Cowley. Wordsworth's opposition of real and
merely poetic language is parallel, and so is Arnold's distinction between Classical and Romantic
styles. One may agree or disagree with the various
applications of this principle, but the principle itself is not affected by them. As soon as it is felt that
a writer is showing off, that he is taking his eye
away from his form and is beginning to introduce
things that he cannot resist, a barrier goes up at
once. The reason is that a self-conscious cleverness
interrupting the unity of the form is an interven-
tion from the ordinary personality, with its claims
to attention, a kind of attempt at direct address
from the author as "man." The barrier is a sign
that direct address, which has no place in literature as such, is being resisted.

In short, "imitation" as a critical conception

becomes nonsense as soon as nature as the content of art is confused or identified with nature conceived as the environment or occasion of art. "Creation" in its turn becomes nonsense as soon as the creator of the poem is confused or identified with the man who also uses words to order his breakfast. Or, more positively, the real meaning and value of both of these essential critical terms are in a conception of literature which distinguishes it from what is not literature.

So far we have been presenting, in summary form, traditional critical conceptions about the process and the product of literature, the *poeta* and the *poema*, to use the traditional terms. What I wish to superimpose on this, and which may be new, is a similar conception of the process and the product of criticism. This new conception means, first of all, that the triangular relationship we originally proposed, with a critic watching the poet and his poem, is inadequate. We need four corners for our palace of art. Just as literature, or the total body of what is produced, is the conception polarizing the writer, so criticism, conceived as the total body of literature as something understood, polarizes the critic.

The first step to take here is to realize that just as a poem implies a distinction between the poet as man and the poet as verbal craftsman, so the response to a poem implies a corresponding distinction in the critic. A critic at a play may have his attention utterly absorbed by the play; but in the intermission, the ordinary personality reappears, takes out the critical personality like a watch, and examines its pointer readings. If the critic has been deeply moved by the play, his critical response will set up an echo in the rest of the personality, but he is never persuaded out of his senses, like Don Quixote at the puppet show. Nor should he be: a "real" or fully engaged response to art does not heighten consciousness but lowers and debases it. Such responses are appealed to by what ought to be absurd, as in naive melodrama, or by the interested, as in propaganda, or by the pornographic, or by the vicious and perverted, as in the various arts of rabble-rousing. We occasionally hear of people who faint or scream at plays: this is always interpreted as a tribute to the vividness of the play, not to their critical sensitivity. We find even famous critics attaching so much importance to admiring some writers and repudiating others that their criticism begins to impress us as a kind of misapplied moral energy rather than actual criticism.

The failure to split the critic off from the rest of the critic's personality produces the associative or stock response, a critical conception established in I. A. Richards' *Practical Criticism*. The stock response, in failing to split the critic, fails also to split either the poet or nature, and so commits both the fallacies described above. When stock response looks at a picture, it cannot see the picture: it can only see the content of the picture as a reproduction of something in external nature, and reacts to its association with the latter. If it is a picture of cows, stock response feels placid, because that is its habitual association with cows: if it is a non-objective painting, stock response says, "Why, that looks like—" and tries to think of something funny that the picture resembles. Mark Twain's comparison of Turner's "Slave Ship" to a tortoise-shell cat having a fit in a platter of tomatoes is a hundred years old, and will do for all similar facetiae. Again, stock response cannot read a poem, but can only react to the content of a poem, which it judges as inspiring or boring or shocking according to its moral anxieties. Stock response is apt to hanker after some form of censorship, for it cannot understand that works of literature can only be good or bad in their own categories, and that no subject-matter or vocabulary is inherently bad.

The most easily corrected type of stock response, perhaps, is the mytho-historical, which is also probably the most common source of stock responses. I had a student once who was shocked to hear me refer to "Good King Wenceslas," at a carol-singing gathering, as a silly poem. Investigation disclosed that he thought it had been written in the thirteenth century, and that anything coming from that age breathed a spirit of the simple piety of an age of faith which, etc., etc.— from there one goes on to St. Thomas Aquinas and the Chartres Cathedral. I explained that this narrative did not come from the thirteenth century, but was a kind of Victorian singing commercial, whereupon he lost all interest in "Good King Wenceslas," because he also held the view that anything written in the mid-nineteenth century was too contemptible for words. Such critical water-wings do no great harm as long as they are eventually dispensed with, but this is only an obviously naive example of a very common form of misplaced concreteness. He had, after all, derived these notions from some book with a butterslide theory of Western culture, according to which this or that spiritual or cultural entity was "lost" after Dante or Raphael or Mozart or whatever the author was attaching his pastoral myth to.

A slightly more difficult type of stock response is the biographical, which assumes that the relation between a poet and his reader is the relation between one man and another, and refuses to read the poet with any admiration if something in his biography, such as his treatment of his wife, seems unsatisfactory. The pseudo-criticism of such poets as Milton and Shelley is strewn with attempts to document a stock response to the poetry by references to the life. Here we may give a more advanced example of a critical fallacy than the previous one. Near the beginning of *Stones of Venice*, Ruskin examines a Renaissance tomb of a doge in a Venetian church, which, as it was placed high up in the church, had been carved only in the parts that could be seen from below, the luckless sculptor not expecting Ruskin to come along centuries later with a sacristan's ladder and descend on it from above, like the Last Judgement. Ruskin works himself into a fine Victorian tantrum over the moral and esthetic dishonesty of the sculptor, and concludes with triumph:

But now, reader, comes the very gist and point of the whole matter: This lying monument to a dishonoured doge, this culminating pride of the Renaissance art of Venice, is at least veracious, if in nothing else, in its testimony to the character of its sculptor. *He was banished from Venice for forgery* in 1497. [Italics, naturally, Ruskin's.]

Ruskin may well be right about the actual merits of the tomb, but that is not always a valid excuse for a wrong critical method, and we need not labor the point that such methods are headed in the direction of more sinister versions of stock response. The next step is the type of pseudo-criticism favored by fascist or communist states, where a poet's merits and characteristics are deduced from whatever seem to have been, after consulting his biography, his social attitudes or ethnical origins. Stock response, then, is ultimately the interference with criticism by what in our first chapter we called the ego, and which finds its fulfillment in the social consensus that we called the mob.

In looking at the relation between the writer and literature as the total body of what writers produce, we found that *poeta* and *poema* are embedded in a common context which critics have almost universally agreed to call nature. If we look at the relation between the critic and literature as the total body of what critics respond to, the common context would be better described as experience, following Aristotle's conception of poetry as a *mimesis praxeos,* an imitation (in words) of human action. The critic, then, is concerned with two kinds of experience. First, he has to understand and interpret the experience which forms the content of the work he is reading. Second, the impact of the literary work on him is itself an experience, "an experience different in kind from any experience not of art," as T. S. Eliot puts it.

The most obvious way of trying to connect these two kinds of experience is to assume that the basis of critical understanding is the resemblance of the experience in the poem to some real experi-

ence the critic has had or could imagine himself
having. Such an assumption is usually founded
on, or develops, a theory of illusion or *Schein*, according to which the literary work manifests a
reality to which the critic discovers a counterpart
in himself. Conceptions of illusion are often used
as the basis of realistic theories. The unities of time
and place in drama have been defended on the
ground that the spectator cannot accept an illusion of time lasting longer than the time he is
sitting in the theatre. The assumption here appears
to be that the illusion must maintain some kind of
proportion to the spectator's own possible experience. The same curious *a posteriori* argument is
applied to the lyric by Poe, who denies that a
genuine experience of poetry can last longer than
a "sitting." One can see from this metaphor that
we are not clear of the stock response: the ordinary personality, which undoubtedly sits, is being
confused with the critical one, which in itself
neither sits nor stands, nor, with Milton's creation,
creeps, walks, swims or flies. Involved here, too,
is a further assumption that those who have had,
or wish to have, or could conceive of themselves
as having, an experience like that of the poem will

understand it better, or "get more out of it," than those who are personally detached from such experience.

Poe's essay, just referred to, quotes Shelley's "I arise from dreams of thee," and says it will be appreciated "by none so thoroughly as by him who has himself arisen from sweet dreams of one beloved, to bathe in the aromatic air of a southern midsummer night." For this poem, therefore, those who have had the somewhat rarefied, if undoubtedly Virginian, experience it describes constitute an inner circle of response. The same kind of critical assumption has in other contexts raised a thick cloud of pseudo-critical issues connected with the problem of poetry and belief. *Paradise Lost*, for instance, presents experiences associated with religious doctrine: hence, so the assumption runs, those who actually believe in a personal devil or in the historical reality of Adam and Eve will find that the poem "means more" to them than if they did not have such beliefs. The conception of literature as an illusion founded on a potential common bond of experience, which looks at first sight like a common-sense theory of art, is really an esoteric one, where each work of art has its inner circle of those who have a special type of contact with the experiences described. Such a critical assumption, then, turns all of literature into various types of allegory, and it divides its audience, as allegory always tends to do, into the initiates and the *profanum vulgus*.

We can see what is wrong with this conception of criticism if we turn to the other form of critical experience, the impact of the poem itself. This is often characterized as a kind of heightening of consciousness which acts chiefly on the emotions, and is, or is closely connected with, pleasure or delight. The Longinian emphasis on sublimity leads to metaphors of "elevation," and this emphasis recurs in later doctrines of the "pleasures of the imagination." In our day we hear about the response of a highly strung nervous system to poetry, in which it is not difficult to see the Romantic metaphor of the Aeolian harp still echoing. The mimetic tradition has always assured us, from Aristotle on, that we, being precocious monkeys, take an inordinate pleasure in seeing things cleverly imitated, or that (as in Locke) perceiving resemblances gives us a pleasure that the analytic habit of perceiving differences cannot supply.

Literature in this aspect is not merely something to admire: like a saddled horse, it increases our own energy and "carries us away."

We discover however that such carriers, like other modes of transport, often lose their efficiency as time goes on: what carried us away at the age of twelve may not take us very far or fast now. Standards of taste in the arts are, it is true, much more flexible than standards of accuracy in science; but, with all allowance made for individual variety, there clearly are such standards. And the theory of direct experience will not lead us to them, for two reasons. First, the reality or intensity of the critic's response does not guarantee that the response itself has any critical validity. Emily Dickinson remarked that if she felt as though the top of her head were taken off, she knew that what she was reading was poetry. But she could only have said this when she had acquired enough maturity to trust such a reaction. One may feel the same way in adolescence about things that one later ranks very low in the scale of values. The immature judgement is based on no less real an experience, but literary experience, at first, is bound to be full of the subjective and private associations of stock response.

If I may be permitted a personal example: in my early days as a graduate student I was assisting the editor of a magazine devoted to poetry, and it was my task to winnow the mail and select what was fit for the editor to read. One poem about flowers was turned in which contained the phrase "golden rain." My critical judgement told me that this poem was of no great merit, but there was something about the phrase "golden rain" that made me feel as though my viscera were floating in space. I finally, after long reflection, realized why: at the age of ten I had set off some fireworks on a holiday, which had given me as intense an esthetic experience as I had ever had, and one of these fireworks bore the title of "golden rain." This purely subjective and associative response did not interfere with my actual critical judgement, but the very fact that it did not was impressive proof that two quite different responses were involved.

The second reason for the inadequacy of the theory of real experience is the haphazard and precarious nature of experience itself. Our moments of intense awareness are not necessarily connected with literature at all; when they are, they are not necessarily right, and when the conditions are right for them, they do not necessarily arise. Apart from the stealthy advance of what we only grudgingly learn to like and the stealthy departure of regretted enthusiasms, we find that the coincidence of great literature with an appropriate response has a large element of accident in it. Many plays are seen in the wrong mood and many poems are read with a headache or with our minds on something else. However, in the general welter of our literary experiences we become aware that in their passing there is also a floundering, spasmodic, inconsistent, yet continual increase of what at length becomes unmistakably a growing body of knowledge. Eventually we may come to understand that it is this body of knowledge which constitutes criticism as such, and not the direct experience of literature. It is knowledge that connects one experience with another, corrects false impressions and inadequacies, and makes possible that progression and sequence in experience without which there could be no such thing as criticism. It was long ago observed by Burke that it is the understanding alone which distinguishes good from bad taste. The presence of criticism as a body of knowledge *democratizes* literature: it provides for literature an educational discipline, something that can be taught and learned; it makes literature accessible to any student with good will, and prevents it from stagnating among groups of mutually unintelligible élites.

This structure of knowledge is all the more essential in criticism, because direct experience, and the intuitions of value it brings, cannot be directly communicated. The kind of "dialogue," as it is now fashionable to call it, that can be established between teacher and student on a basis of experience and value-judgement alone is not helpful. Thus: (Teacher) Yeats's *Among School Children* is one of the great poems of the twentieth century. (Student) But I don't like it; it seems to me a lot of clap-trap; I get a lot more out of *The Cremation of Sam McGee.* (Teacher) The answer is simple: your taste is inferior to mine. (Student) But how do you know it's inferior? (Teacher) I just know, that's all. All teaching of literature is based on the indefinite postponing of this dialogue until the student learns enough about literature, as an ordered body of knowledge, to sing a more harmonious antiphony. For the values we want the student to acquire from us cannot be taught: only knowledge of literature can be taught. Without the possibility of criticism as a structure of knowledge, culture, and society with it, would be forever condemned to a morbid antagonism between the supercilious refined and the resentful unrefined.

II

THE study of literature as an object of understanding, and the experience of literature as an object of wonder and admiration, are, of course, different things. Experience, for one thing, avoids repetition: we do not want two tremendous experiences of *King Lear* in the same day—hardly even in the same year. The study of the play, ransacking its text and comparing Folio and Quarto versions, is clearly something quite different even from the kind of experience described by Keats in his sonnet on rereading *King Lear*. Some people feel that study may blunt the edge of experience, or, as they often say, that it will kill a poem to analyze it. It is possible for someone naturally insensitive to become more so through familiarity, but this fear in itself is a superstition based on another critical fallacy related to the stock response but different in context. This is the fallacy of separating the understanding of literature from the appreciation of it. All fallacies of separation have two aspects. If we think of literature in purely esthetic and hieratic terms, we think of the end of criticism as a vision of beauty; if we think of it in purely oratorical and demotic terms, we think of the end of criticism as a possession of some form of imaginative truth. Beauty and truth are certainly relevant to the study of literature, but if either is separated from the other and made an end in itself, something goes wrong.

The direct experience of literature is usually thought of as a heightening of consciousness accompanied by pleasure. This conception is closely related to the Platonic view that ordinary experience, on its subject-object level, is distinguishable from a higher experience, where subject and object have become love and beauty respectively. The language of criticism, whenever it speaks of sublimity and the like, is frequently close to erotic language. We are not surprised to find that Shelley, with his Platonic leanings, identifies love and art, and bases his criticism on the superiority of this kind of consciousness to the ordinary discursive subject-object kind. Not far from Plato, too, is the assumption that the theory of art has a particularly close relationship to the theory of beauty. This assumption seems almost to be involved in the very existence of "esthetics" as a branch of philosophy. Yet beauty can be predicated of many things besides art, and surely any conception of it which brings works of art into *direct* competition with girls in bathing suits ought to be looked at with some suspicion. There is, certainly, an important analogy between the esthetic contemplation of a work of art and the "delight" or "pleasure" which catches our attention in nature. Whether this analogy will hold up a complete theory of art or not is another matter.

In ordinary speech, the word "beautiful" soon comes to mean, not a quality or effect of the unity of form, but a stock response to content. That is, "beautiful" usually means possessing attractive subject-matter, a synonym of loveliness. Hence such words as "instruction" or "truth" have regularly been added in order to get some roughage in the cultural diet. In conversation, at least, the word beauty is normally excluded from any serious discussion of art. We say that in Dickens such characters as Chadband or Micawber are better done, more vivid, representative of a more significant part of Dickens's genius, than his unmemorably lovely heroines. But it is hard to say how we could call either the characters or Dickens's treatment of them more "beautiful" without doing some violence to ordinary language. The word ugliness is equally confused. If it were a genuinely critical term, many a calendar picture of a pretty girl with thirty-two teeth and no clothes would be instantly called ugly. But we seldom use the word in this sense: we tend to reserve it either for dramatically unfashionable taste or for representations of repellent subject-matter. In the nineteenth century there was some attempt to distinguish the artist who portrayed the "ugly" and didn't like doing it from the artist who portrayed it and did, the former producing a healthy and the latter a morbid form of grotesque. Which was which could be decided subjectively or, again, biographically.

This notion still survives as a stock response. The colloquial debasing of such words is not, of course, a serious argument against their proper use; but there is something in the words themselves that seems to throw us off the rails.

We arrive at similar frustrations in pursuit of truth. The fundamental act of criticism is a disinterested response to a work of literature in which all one's beliefs, engagements, commitments, prejudices, stampedings of pity and terror, are ordered to be quiet. We are now dealing with the imaginative, not the existential, with "let this be," not with "this is," and no work of literature is better by virtue of what it says than any other work. Such a disinterested response takes rigorous discipline to attain, and many, even among skilled critics, never consistently attain it. But the fact that it is there to be attained can hardly be disputed. At the same time such detachment is not an end in itself. We still have our engagements and commitments, our beliefs, our ideals, and what we may call our habitual imaginative attitudes; and it is natural to have a special enthusiasm for whatever expresses them well in literature. The feeling that there is such a thing as imaginative truth cannot be easily dismissed, and literature that seems to us "true" in this more specific sense is literature we feel we can trust: it participates in our lives and we in its articulateness. The demotic or oratorical aspect of literature, in which it is a spokesman for our own ideals and attitudes, is a genuine aspect. It is not necessarily naive to write "how true" on the margins of what we read; or at least we do not have to confine our contact with literature to purely disinterested and esthetic responses. We should mutilate our literary experience if we did, and mutilations of experience designed merely to keep a theory consistent indicate something wrong with the theory.

To go beyond this point would take us into a world of higher belief, a view of the human situation so broad that the whole of literature would illustrate it. But clearly no axioms of such a view could be formulated: all formulations would either have to be too narrow to apply to the whole of literature, or too vague to have definite meaning. Beauty and truth may be attributes of good writing, but if the writer deliberately aims at truth, he is likely to find that what he has hit is the didactic; if he deliberately aims at beauty, he is likely to find that what he has hit is the insipid. The poet, rather, writes out what takes shape in his mind, and works with such categories as unity, consistency, and appropriateness or decorum. If he says what should be said at that point, its beauty and truth will take care of themselves. Beauty then means the strength and accuracy of the creative energy, or, as Blake says, exuberance is beauty. Truth means what is true for that place, such as the blasphemies of Milton's Satan and the hallucinations of Don Quixote. Criticism must shape its categories in the same way. Whether we regard literature as a transparent medium of a higher truth or as a beautiful end in itself, we are remaining on the level of a detached contemplative view of human artifacts, a view which is idolatrous to its own shadow, to quote Blake again. We said in the first chapter that the end of literary education is an ethical and participating aim, the transfer of imaginative energy from writer to reader, but we have not yet found the means to this end.

The traditional attitude to the arts that Arnold associated with the term "Hebraism" distrusts beauty because its standards are so elusive compared to the impersonal truth of moral and intellectual law. Hence it regards the arts, including literature, as deriving what value they have from their approximation to such law. For the "Hebraist," moral and intellectual law is the direct or primary form of God's revelation to man and accommodation to man's mind. The arts are thus to be regarded as allegories of truth, and judged accordingly. This conception is closely related to the one just dealt with, that a work of literature is an allegory of a real experience common to itself and to its critic. Since Arnold's time the "Hebraic" attitude has dropped its God and become the attitude of Marxism, for which again the arts are allegories of "social realism." This is historically a development of the demotic or Longinian tradition that revived with Romanticism, which may be one reason why art in Marxist countries exhibits Romantic and even Victorian affinities. Being demotic, it is addressed to the people, but being also essentially allegorical, it soon finds within itself an inner circle of people who understand how social realism is to be interpreted at the time.

The modern non-Marxist reader is not likely to need warnings against the inadequacy of this approach to criticism. The bourgeois world has tended rather toward a hieratic or formalist view of the arts which, at least in the beginning, laid great stress on its anti-Romantic and neo-Classical ("Hellenist") bias. This approach, without making much explicit use of the terms truth and beauty, divides the mind into an intellect concerned with truth and an emotion which seeks the emotional equivalents or correlatives of truth, whose statements are pseudo-statements and provide, as Aristotle said of rhetoric, an answering chorus to truth. The arts are assigned to this emotional category.

As we are looking for a more unified conception of criticism than either of these approaches provides, we need an approach that does not try to split up the mind, or ignore the obvious fact that both intellect and emotion are fully and simultaneously involved in all our literary experience. In our present terminology, then, we can say that there is a study of literature, or criticism proper, and there is a direct experience of literature. These are the critical equivalents of the search for truth and the search for beauty respectively. These two are, in the first place, inseparable, two halves of one great whole which is the *possession* of literature. The study of literature purifies our experience of the private and irrelevant associations of stock response. The more we know about literature, the better the chances that intensity of response and the greatness of the stimulus to it will coincide. An increasingly sensitive experience of literature, on the other hand, purifies the study of literature of pedantry, or literary experience without any depth of emotional content.

The relation between literature and the informative or discursive verbal disciplines, philosophy, history, the social sciences, literary criticism itself, is involved at this point, but I have space only to consider this question in its abstract or simplified form of the relation between literature and belief.

As something produced, the poem is a man-made thing (*techne*) to be distinguished from other things we see in the world around us. In this context, the poem is a form that has "nature" for its content, the nature which is the content of the poem being split off from the nature which is the environment of the poem. As something understood or experienced, the poem is a human endeavor, to be distinguished from other aspects of human experience and action. In this context the poem is a form that has human experience or action for its content, which is similarly to be split off from real experience or real action. Real human action expresses, consciously or unconsciously, certain axioms, beliefs or convictions which can be given some verbal formulation. The more highly developed one's life, the more consistently one's beliefs find expression in action, and the more completely one's real beliefs can be reconstructed from one's behavior. Such a life is the life of practical reason we spoke of in the first chapter, where *quid credas* passes into *quid agas*, and the detached categories of truth and falsehood become the engaged categories of freedom and restriction. In all Marxist and in much hieratic criticism, literature is enlisted in the operation of carrying beliefs into action, either directly as propaganda or indirectly by aligning the emotions with what the intellect sees to be the right course of action. Both forms of criticism are intensely conservative, though what they wish to conserve naturally differs: revolutionary dogma for one and some more traditional social or religious dogma for the other.

In both these views the individual work of literature is related first of all to the experience which is beyond, behind or manifested in it, whether we apprehend that experience allegorically or formally, intellectually or emotionally. Literary experiences, according to this, are discrete: what holds them together is something other than literature, whether our emotional life or our view of society. I suggest, on the other hand, that the first thing for *criticism* to do with any literary experience, the first step in understanding it as literature, is to associate it with other literary experiences. If a student is reading *Lycidas* or Shakespeare's sonnets, he naturally tries first of all to read them allegorically, as disguised transcripts of real experiences with Edward King or Mr. W. H. If he fails, he will protest that they must be mere literary exercises, with no "real feeling" in them. It is of course only the inexperienced student who does this. The experienced and patient teacher must show him that Lycidas is a literary figure in a family of literary pastorals, whose next of kin are in Theocritus and Virgil and not in seventeenth-century Cambridge; that the only relevant experiences Milton had are his previous efforts in the pastoral convention; that the only relevant feelings he had are concerned with his determination to do a good job with a pastoral elegy. Shakespeare's beautiful youth is another literary figure, an Eros or Hermaphroditus, and belongs in the literary convention of love poetry.

Similarly with our own experience. It is legitimate enough to associate the characters we meet in modern plays and novels with people we know, or to wonder whether in real life people would behave like the characters in the fiction. We often feel with delight that this is exactly the way people are, that this is a clairvoyantly true observation of human life. Such a feeling is really a feeling of coordination, a sense that literature is uniting a great number of possible real experiences in a single insight. The study of literature takes the direction of making this feeling more precise and systematic. Our literary understanding of a character does not begin until we associate him with other literary characters. The more we know about literature, the more clearly its interconnecting structural principles appear: the conventions that link characters in O'Casey with characters of the same type and function in Aristophanes; the genres common to Shakespeare and Sophocles, to Proust and Lady Murasaki; the myths that connect contemporary poets with ancient classics. We have always been told that the function of literature is to instruct and delight, but only when we try to locate our literary experiences within literature do these two things become one thing.

In this process, literature as a whole is independent of real experience and something distinct from the passing of belief into action. Literature is a body of hypothetical thought and action: it makes, as literature, no statements or assertions. It neither reflects nor escapes from the world of belief and action, but contains it in its own distinctive form. It is this independence from real experience which the term "imagination" expresses, a term which includes both intellect and emotion, and yet is different from actual truth or real feelings. When we meet an unfamiliar experience in literature, the relevant question is not, is this true? but, is it imaginatively conceivable? If not, there is still a chance that our notion of what is imaginatively conceivable needs expanding. Literature thus provides a kind of reservoir of possibilities of action. It gives us wider sympathies and greater tolerance, and new perspectives on action; it increases the power of articulating convictions, whether our own or those of others.

Between imagination and belief there is constant traffic in both directions. Gods that men no longer believe in become literary characters; philosophical systems that are now only constructs become extensions of literary culture; political loyalties that have lost their context in society fall back into the imagination that conceived them. They take on a new life when they lose their power to direct or express the direction of action, but it is a different kind of life. We also see new beliefs emerging from the imaginative world, as they did from the writings of Rousseau in the eighteenth century. As long as both imagination and belief are working properly, we can avoid the neurotic extremes of the dilettante who is so bemused by imaginative possibilities that he has no convictions, and the bigot who is so bemused by his convictions that he cannot see them as also possibilities. But it is clear that imagination and belief have different functions, and it is unfortunate that Arnold should have spoken of poetry or culture as substituting for or coming to replace belief, as this is a red herring in criticism. A belief can only be replaced by another belief, even when a godless religion is substituted for a godly one.

The relation of imagination and belief raises once again the question of high style. We recall that high demotic style has a close connection with the proverb and the aphorism, the axiom of behavior. We read literature with our own axioms of behavior and belief already in existence, and we have high demotic style when something in our reading strikes an echo in our habitual attitudes. The direction of high demotic style is thus centrifugal: it travels outward from the imaginative into the "real" world. We notice that proverbial and sententious statements in poetry have a curiously anonymous quality about them and come loose very easily from their context. Many people are familiar with "A little learning is a dangerous thing" and "The course of true love never did run smooth" who know nothing of the *Essay on Criticism* or *A Midsummer Night's Dream.* Sometimes what we read is known to be a source of our convictions, as the Gospels would be for a Christian or the Communist Manifesto for a Marxist. But even here the instinct to "apply" what we read, to lead a passage out of its original context into that of our own affairs, is very strong.

High hieratic style, on the other hand, is centripetal in direction, and demands to be kept in its original context. The line "And what is else not to be overcome" is one of Arnold's touchstones, but we can hardly see it as one without putting it where it belongs, in Satan's speech in the first book of *Paradise Lost*. Once there, the attribute of high style spreads over the whole passage, then over most of the book, until we are in possession of the entire epic; nor does the process stop there. We feel that we are in the presence of high style in this mode when what we read suddenly becomes a focus of our whole literary experience and imaginative life, when we feel that this is the kind of thing that literature can do, and has done for us. Arnold's Aristotelian phrase "high seriousness," and his tendency to find his touchstones in epic and tragedy, suggest that high style is invariably solemn; but it can equally well be a flash of wit or ribaldry. Our own conceptions of both forms of high style are subject to improvement. The inexperienced student may find high demotic style in

cliché, accepted idea and the stimuli of stock response; a teenager may find high hieratic style in
a Tin Pan Alley lyric. It is fortunate that education
in such matters is possible; but the principles of
such education are a sealed book to critics as yet,
and I can see only one more step to take before I
must abandon this argument.

So far we have been speaking of "the critic," as
though the response to poetry were individual;
but, of course, it is social as well. The social response is most obvious in the theatre, but it holds
for all genres: we cannot become the exclusive pos-
sessors of a book of poems by buying it, as we may
with a painting. The creation of literature may
be and often is a lonely process, but the response
to it becomes increasingly a community of understanding, a sharing of vision. Literature, therefore,
must relate itself ultimately to some kind of human community. As a disinterested world in which
anything is conceivable and nothing really happens, it is in the individual mind the place of seed
from which all conscious action is born and to
which it returns, a world where, as Blake says of
Beulah, no dispute can come. But in society it is
the real parliament of man, the deliberative body

in the center, the symposium which in Plato is the model of society, the academic vision of possibilities which is the model of education. It is unfortunate that to speak of "the republic of letters," or to associate liberal education with social freedom, should suggest only the rhetoric of commencement addresses and not functional conceptions in critical theory. But it seems clear that Arnold was on solid ground when he made "culture," a total imaginative vision of life with literature at its center, the regulating and normalizing element in social life, the human source, at least, of spiritual authority. Culture in Arnold's sense is the exact opposite of an élite's game preserve; it is, in its totality, a vision or model of what humanity is capable of achieving, the matrix of all Utopias and social ideals. It does not amuse: it educates, hence it acts as an informing principle in ordinary life, dissolving the inequalities of class structure and the dismal and illiberal ways of life that arise when society as a whole does not have enough vision.

When we speak of actual human life, or the actual environment of nature, we speak of something of which literature is only a part, and a ridiculously small part at that. But when we speak of literature, we speak of a total imaginative form which is, in that context, *bigger* than either nature or human life, because it contains them, the actual being only a part of the possible. There is an eloquent passage in Longinus which explains how the whole universe is insufficient to meet the demands of poets, and Bacon remarks in the *Advancement of Learning* that this is why the arts have been so constantly associated with divinity. Literature, we say, neither reflects nor escapes from ordinary life: what it does reflect is the world as human imagination conceives it, in mythical, romantic, heroic and ironic as well as realistic and fantastic terms. This world is the universe in human form, stretching from the complete fulfillment of human desire to what human desire utterly repudiates, the *quo tendas* vision of reality that elsewhere I have called, for reasons rooted in my study of Blake, apocalyptic. In this world the difference between the two kinds of high style just mentioned disappears.

Some religions assume that such a world exists, though only for gods; other religions, including those closer to us, identify it with a world man enters at death, the extremes of desire becoming its heavens and hells; revolutionary philosophies associate it with what man is to gain in the future; mystics call it the world of total or cosmic consciousness. A poet may accept any of these identifications without damage to his poetry; but for the literary critic, this larger world is the world that man exists and participates in through his imagination. It is the world in which our imaginations move and have their being while we are also living in the "real" world, where our imaginations find the ideals that they try to pass on to belief and action, where they find the vision which is the source of both the dignity and the joy of life. High style, whether demotic or hieratic, is the authentic speech of that world, the language which is neither impersonal nor spoken by this or that person, but the language of humanity itself.

Notes

(These notes are designed only to correct some over-allusiveness in the text: many of them may be superfluous.)

PAGE

15 "Pope." *Essay on Criticism*, 292.

37 "Kierkegaard." *Concluding Unscientific Postscript*, tr. David Swenson and Walter Lowrie (1941), 115 ff.

41 "Mencken." In *The American Language*, more or less *passim*.

48–9 The tags *quid credas, quid agas,* and *quo tendas* (what you should believe, what you should do, where you should be going) were used in the Middle Ages to describe the three levels of meaning beyond the literal level: the allegorical, the moral or tropological, and the anagogic. Cf. Dante's *Convivio*, II, i, and Francis Fergusson, *Dante's Drama of the Mind* (1953), 179.

51 "Satan." *Paradise Lost*, i, 650.

57 The line of Pope's is from *The Dunciad*, i, 32.

61–4 The quotations from sixteenth and seventeenth-century writers have been modernized.

64 "Falstaff." Cf. *Henry IV, Part One*, II, iv, 374 ff. Euphuism derives its name from Lyly's *Euphues,* referred to below.

68 "Coleridge." The poem is called "Reflections on Having Left a Place of Retirement." When originally published it bore the additional subtitle: "A Poem which affects not to be Poetry." The phrase *sermoni propriora,* from Horace's *Satires,* I, iv, 42, means "closer to ordinary conversation" (or to prose, as *sermo* does not make the distinction I am trying to establish in the text). Charles Lamb's translation, "more proper for a sermon," has much to be said for it.

(1864), Bagehot quotes the following passage from "Enoch Arden":

> While Enoch was abroad on wrathful seas,
> Or often journeying landward; for in truth
> Enoch's white horse, and Enoch's ocean spoil
> In ocean-smelling osier, and his face,
> Rough-redden'd with a thousand winter gales,
> Not only to the market-cross were known,
> But in the leafy lanes behind the down,
> Far as the portal-warding lion-whelp,
> And peacock yew-tree of the lonely Hall,
> Whose Friday fare was Enoch's ministering.

and remarks, "So much has not often been made of selling fish."

100 "Blake once suggested." Cf. *Public Address*, Rossetti MS., 18–19. For the formulaic epic cf. Albert B. Lord, *The Singer of Tales* (1960).

103 "Joyce." A concise explanation of the term "epiphany" in Joyce may be found in Theodore Spencer's introduction to *Stephen Hero* (1944), 16 ff.

104 " 'purple patch.' " Horace, *Ars Poetica*, 15–16. The context in Horace is one of parody, but the phrase has been extended, usually in the form "purple passage," to more favorable senses.

104 "It was Poe." All references to Poe's critical theory are to his essay *The Poetic Principle*.

104 "Valéry's phrase." *The Art of Poetry*, 23.

106 "Arnold's 'touchstones.' " See his essay *The Study of Poetry*, reprinted in *Essays in Criticism*, Second Series.

115 "Croce's term." Cf. *Aesthetic*, tr. Douglas Ainslie (rev. ed. 1922), ch. i.

116 "Coleridge." From his essay *On Poesy or Art*.

116 *"ut pictura poesis."* Horace, *Ars Poetica*, 361: cf. *Elizabethan Critical Essays*, ed. Gregory Smith, Vol. I, 386.

PAGE

117 "Eliot." Cf. *Selected Essays* (3rd ed., 1951), 242.

120 "metaphors of relaxed will." Cf. Wordsworth, Preface to *Lyrical Ballads;* Keats, Letter to George and Thomas Keats, Dec. 1817; Eliot, "Tradition and the Individual Talent."

120 "Longinus." *On the Sublime,* xviii.

120 "assumed to have a virtue." The references are to Johnson's *Life of Cowley;* Coleridge's *Biographia Literaria,* ch. iv; Wordsworth's Preface; Arnold's Preface to the *Poems* of 1853.

122 "the *poeta* and the *poema.*" Cf. Spingarn, *Critical Essays of the Seventeenth Century,* Vol. I, 226–7. The third traditional term, *poesis,* is what is meant here by criticism.

128 "T. S. Eliot." "Tradition and the Individual Talent" (*Selected Essays,* 18).

129 "Poe." The references are again to *The Poetic Principle.*

132 "Emily Dickinson." Reported in T. W. Higginson's article on her in the *Atlantic Monthly,* 1891.

135 "Burke." From the Essay on Taste which introduces his treatise *On the Sublime and Beautiful.*

142 "to quote Blake again." *Jerusalem,* Plate 29.

142 "Arnold." The terms "Hebraism" and "Hellenism" are in *Culture and Anarchy,* ch. iv.

144 "Aristotle." The opening sentence of Aristotle's treatise on rhetoric states that "Rhetoric is the counterpart (*antistrophos*) of dialectic."

150 "Arnold." From *The Study of Poetry,* as before.

153 "as Blake says of Beulah." Cf. Blake, *Milton,* Plate 33.

154 "symposium." Cf. Plato, *Laws,* Books i and ii.

154 "Arnold." *Culture and Anarchy,* ch. i.

155 "Longinus." *On the Sublime,* xxxv.

155 "Bacon." Cf. Spingarn, *op. cit.,* I, 6.